ESSAYS ON RADICALISM IN CONTEMPORARY AMERICA

THE WALTER PRESCOTT WEBB MEMORIAL LECTURES: VI

THE WALTER PRESCOTT WEBB MEMORIAL LECTURES

ESSAYS ON RADICALISM IN CONTEMPORARY AMERICA

BY

JEROME L. RODNITZKY

FRANK ROSS PETERSON

KENNETH R. PHILP

JOHN A. GARRATY

Introduction by Lyndon Baines Johnson

Edited by
Leon Borden Blair

PUBLISHED FOR THE UNIVERSITY OF TEXAS AT ARLINGTON
BY THE UNIVERSITY OF TEXAS PRESS, AUSTIN & LONDON

Library of Congress Cataloging in Publication Data
Main entry under title:

Essays on radicalism in contemporary America.

   (The Walter Prescott Webb memorial lectures: 6)
   Includes bibliographical references.
   1. Radicalism—U. S.—Addresses, essays, lectures.
2. Truman, Harry S., Pres. U. S., 1884–
3. Collier, John, 1884–1968. 4. Depressions—1929—
Addresses, essays, lectures. I. Rodnitzky, Jerome L.,
1936– II. Blair, Leon Borden, 1917– ed.
III. Series.
E169.12.E85   917.3′03′9   75-38237
ISBN 0-292-77001-4

Manufactured in the United States of America
Second Printing, 1973

CONTENTS

Preface ix

Introduction: Lyndon Baines Johnson xiii

Popular Music as a Radical Influence, 1945–1970 . . 3
    JEROME L. RODNITZKY

Harry S. Truman and His Critics: The 1948 Progressives
    and the Origins of the Cold War 32
    FRANK ROSS PETERSON

John Collier and the American Indian, 1920–1945 . 63
    KENNETH R. PHILP

Radicalism in the Great Depression 81
    JOHN A. GARRATY

PREFACE

In the sixth annual Walter Prescott Webb Memorial Lectures, held at The University of Texas at Arlington on April 22, 1971, four historians have examined various aspects of radicalism. Despite differences in background, their judgments are remarkably consistent.

Jerome L. Rodnitzky, thirty-five, a Midwesterner, with a 1966 Ph.D. degree from the University of Chicago, has considered the social impact of radicalism as expressed in popular music which, he says, has played an important role during the past twenty-five years in developing a radical mentality, particularly among young people. But he found that the aggregate impact of the protest singers was a sort of "communal euphoria," and that, although most of them left the lockstep of "the protest biz," they bequeathed "examples of conscience and principle to a society which has increasingly been unable to provide its young with credible examples of either conscience or principle.

Frank Ross Peterson, twenty-nine, a Westerner, with a Ph.D. degree from Washington State University (1968), found his topic in political radicalism in the West. He examined the ineffectual protests of Glen Taylor and Henry Wallace and the

Progressive party of 1948. Both Taylor and Wallace sang the
same reform-minded isolationist song, Wallace through the editorial pages of the *New Republic*, and Taylor from the floor of
the United States Senate. Both based their arguments on that old
bugaboo of the 1930's, the "big figures in the finance and business world" who sought to manipulate United States foreign
policy to serve "private corporations and international big business." Both were overwhelmingly rejected at the polls.

Kenneth R. Philp, thirty, another Midwesterner, with a Ph.D.
degree (1968) from Michigan State University, dealt with the
quest of Indian Commissioner John Collier for a New Deal for
the Indians. Collier was able to reverse almost a half century of
Indian policy, the objective of which had been to turn the Indian
into a white man. In preserving the Indian as an Indian, Collier
helped him to regain his pride in race and culture, showed him
how to compete on the white man's terms—and succeed. The end
result may well be an objective proclaimed but never achieved by
earlier Indian policies: an Indian society which can coexist with
the white communities surrounding it.

John A. Garraty, fifty, Brooklyn-born, with a Ph.D. from Columbia University in 1948, and on its faculty since 1959, looked
at radicalism as a worldwide phenomenon of the Great Depression. Intimately associated with the Eastern Establishment
most of his life, he might well have interpreted radicalism in a
different vein; but he, too, found radicalism to be an evolutionary
rather than a revolutionary influence, particularly in the United
States, but also to a degree in Europe. He found radical leaders
subdued by responsibility and moving toward the traditional, despite their earlier pronouncements. He found radicalism blunted
by patriotism. He concluded that adversity may produce sporadic
violence but it may also awaken the human spirit and develop a
sense of community between those suffering and those more
fortunate.

Examination of these several aspects, by scholars from widely differing fields, indicates that radicalism's pejorative connotation may be undeserved. Perhaps it is after all the root that gives sustenance to the tree of our society.

LEON BORDEN BLAIR

INTRODUCTION

Like most things, radicalism is a matter of perspective; a perspective that is greatly influenced by time and events. And yet, the most obvious characteristic of radicalism is its insistence on immediacy—immediate change, immediate reform, immediate action.

Based on the viewpoint of the present, this insistence on immediacy of change could even be judged as revolutionary. But as the viewpoint of the present becomes the viewpoint of the past, *insistence* on change becomes *persistence* on change—and the "radical" becomes the "reformist," or at times, even the defender of the status quo. In the 1930's, for example, supporters of Social Security and rural electrification were considered by many to be "radical socialists." Today, however, the man who advocated doing away with those programs would be considered radical.

Not all radicals, certainly, are to be taken seriously. Some are merely intellectual gadflies, advocating immediate and sweeping change merely for the sake of change. History is usually quite harsh on those individuals who never settled on an idea long enough to refine it or see it through.

But if one digs a bit deeper, below the superficial layer of the past, he will find that some of these "believers in new and better ideas" were very successful in accomplishing their goals. As this kind of "radical" sees his ideas through to realization, he loses his identity as a radical. He becomes something else in the popular view—an idealist, a humanitarian. Walter Prescott Webb was an example of the latter.

Webb's ideas were unquestionably radical. In the political arena, he refused to accept the status quo, and, in *Divided We Stand*, he made his most eloquent plea for sweeping changes in our political-economic structure.

For Walter Prescott Webb the wheel has turned full circle. Many of his dreams have been realized. His ideas, once so controversial, have been generally accepted, if not always approved. He has made his place as an eminent historian whose ideas have shaped the society in which he lived and for which he dreamed great dreams. I had the privilege to know Professor Webb for more than a quarter century, and have watched the transformation.

Yet many of Webb's ideas have not been realized, and because of his unfortunate and untimely death in 1963, he will not be able to develop the new themes which will shape the future of mankind—as Arnold J. Toynbee suggests that he would have done if he had lived. It is more than appropriate, therefore, that The University of Texas at Arlington should provide a forum for exploring a broad sweep of ideas, and call it the Walter Prescott Webb Memorial Lectures. No memorial could be more fitting.

LYNDON B. JOHNSON

ESSAYS ON RADICALISM IN CONTEMPORARY AMERICA

POPULAR MUSIC
AS A RADICAL INFLUENCE, 1945-1970

□□□□□□□□□□□□□□□□□□□□□□□□□□□□□□

BY JEROME L. RODNITZKY

To TALK OF "RADICAL INFLUENCE" in contemporary America invites visions of stealthy conspirators, drugged fanatics, and wild-eyed terrorists. Increasingly, many Americans insist that what is most vivid must be representative. However, America's radical tradition can neither be erased by emotion nor overwhelmed by headlines. That tradition has a long, honorable history and its proponents, from Roger Williams to Henry Thoreau to David Harris, have a prominent place among American folk heroes. American radicals have always been preoccupied with fundamental reform. Thus, dictionaries frequently define *radical* in terms of its derivation (from *radix*, or root), as an adjective signifying reform that goes to "the root or origin" of a problem.[1]

In the past, radicals usually confronted society with its seamiest aspects and often demanded immediate changes through di-

[1] *The American College Dictionary* (New York: Random House, 1966).

rect action. This has always upset many Americans and tended to
make radicals unpopular. Like the proverbial messenger with bad
news, the radical seldom received an enthusiastic reception. Yet,
those who disturb others are not necessarily all radicals. Blowing
up buildings does not make one a radical, nor does proclaiming
revolution; nor, needless to say, does drug-taking or hair length
qualify one. The radical is characterized by visions of a future
society and by his own rational plans to bring his dreams to
fruition. Thus, in youth's idiom, a radical is not merely turned
off; he must be turned on to alternatives.[2]

Yet, within this classic intellectual tradition, important new
trends are emerging. Historically, the conservative Right cele-
brated the social status quo, while the radical Left sought new
alternatives. In twentieth-century America, this has usually meant
concerted efforts to preserve the capitalist system against socialist onslaughts. However, since 1945, the divisions between Left
and Right have steadily blurred, as both sides became more dissatisfied. The Right has continued to attack society as decadent
and proto-socialist, while the Left has begun to criticize welfare-
state bureaucracy and to demand "participatory democracy," a
trend no doubt fostered by the intellectual dominance of so-called
liberalism in our media and universities. As New Deal liberalism
grew quantitatively, it often declined qualitatively and constituted
a loose ideological shelter for many defenders of the status quo.
Thus, inevitably, radicals rejected the old political boundaries
and moved into the ideological vacuum from both sides. It is no
accident that Ayn Rand's conservative objectivists see themselves
as radicals. Increasingly, diverse groups profoundly disturbed by

---

[2] For an interesting discussion of the intellectual meaning of radicalism, see Daniel Boorstin, "The New Barbarians," *Esquire,* October,
1968, pp. 159–162. For an English view of American radicalism, see
T. B. Bottomore, *Critics of Society: Radical Thought in North America*
(New York: Random House, 1966).

society seek a radical identity. For example, a California-based evangelical group calls itself "The Christian World Liberation Front" and is proud to have its missionaries called "Radicals for Jesus" or even "Jesus Freaks."[3]

While American radicalism has undergone this recent transformation, popular music has played an important role in the development of a radical mentality, especially with youth. American music has seldom been a forum for serious social debate; but the last twenty-five years have produced a revolution in popular music as vast numbers of "protest songs" and "message songs" have penetrated mass culture. Like most revolutions, this phenomenon is less revolutionary than it appears. Protest music has always been with us, but there is a natural tendency to neglect its past. History is usually rosier in perspective and yesterday's protest song becomes increasingly irrelevant. Since topical songs are, by definition, custom-made for a particular time and place, they remain rigid period pieces.[4] However, the most important changes in contemporary message music are its pervasiveness, its technological vividness, and its ability to influence the youthful masses.

Another new development is the new music's often frank political agitation. Such agitation can be simply defined as "persistent urging of a political or social question before the public." What better way to reach the public—especially the young public—than on the proverbial "wings of song"? For, as Alexander Pope observed: "What will a child learn sooner than a song?" And did not Henry Thoreau label music "the arch-reformer"? More directly, Jeremy Collier, a seventeenth-century Englishman, argued that music was "almost as dangerous as gunpowder" and might

[3] George Cornell, "Radicals for Jesus Make Campus Scene," Associated Press story in *Fort Worth Star-Telegram*, June 13, 1970.

[4] See Jerome L. Rodnitzky, "The Evolution of the American Protest Song," *Journal of Popular Culture* 3 (Summer, 1969): 35–36.

require "looking after no less than the press."[5] With these testimonials, it is little wonder that in 1968 Frank Zappa, lead singer of "The Mothers of Invention," asserted that music could help engineer a painless revolution, rather than a blood-in-the-street uprising, by perfecting the advertising techniques that Madison Avenue used to sell washing machines. Zappa expected to "use the system against itself to purge itself" and argued that his music was "constructive," since it supplied "therapeutic shock-waves."[6] Even putting aside these grandiose claims for the moment, it is likely that presently no group of writers, teachers, or preachers can rival songwriters in communicating with youth.

Ironically, the first organized musical efforts to radicalize Americans were aimed strictly at adult workers. The Industrial Workers of the World, founded in Chicago in 1904 and better known as the Wobblies, formed America's most militant labor group. The IWW proposed to organize every worker into a single union and then call a general strike to determine whether bosses or workers would run the world. While pursuing this goal, the Wobblies effectively used blunt protest songs to foster worker solidarity. Writers like Joe Hill and Ralph Chaplin freely borrowed ideas, melodies, and lyrics and blended them into the Wobblies' revolutionary idiom. Thus, the music of "The Battle Hymn of the Republic," became the tune for "Solidarity Forever"—the Wobbly anthem, and Joe Hill made the classic folk song "Casey Jones" into a timely protest ballad by converting Casey from a heroic Illinois Central engineer to a strikebreaking scab for the Southern Pacific. The IWW soon gave a *Little Red Songbook* to new members along with their union card, and on

---

[5] Jeremy Collier, *A Short View of Immorality and the Profaneness of the English State* (London, 1698), Introduction.

[6] Frank Kofsky, "Frank Zappa Interview," in *The Age of Rock*, edited by Jonathan Eisen (New York: Random House, 1969), pp. 255–256.

each red cover appeared the motto: "To Fan the Flames of Discontent." One stanza of "Solidarity Forever" summed up the IWW message neatly:

> They have taken untold millions
>   that they never toiled to earn.
> But without our brain and muscle
>   not a single wheel can turn.
> We can break their haughty power;
>   gain our freedom when we learn
> That the Union makes us strong
> Solidarity forever
> Solidarity forever
> Solidarity forever
> For the union makes us strong.[7]

The IWW was destroyed by its opposition to World War I and the general hysteria against radicals in the war's aftermath, but the new labor unions of the depression-stricken thirties continued the protest-song tradition. Along with the organizing drives of the CIO and United Mine Workers came a flood of protest parodies and new songs celebrating worker unity. Once again laborers sang on the picket lines and in the union halls. However, workers only sing under stress, and long-term prosperity and suburban living have steadily made union songs irrelevant. Except for such very recently organized groups as farm workers, labor unions are no longer singing movements.[8]

Nevertheless, the union song established a precedent and deeply influenced Woody Guthrie, the father of the contemporary

[7] Reprinted in *I.W.W. Songs*, thirty-second edition (Chicago: Industrial Workers of the World, 1968), p. 10.

[8] Rodnitzky, "The Evolution of the American Protest Song," pp. 36–38. For an excellent and detailed account of the history of American protest songs, see John Greenway, *American Folksongs of Protest* (Philadelphia: University of Pennsylvania Press, 1953).

protest ballad. Guthrie, a restless folk singer from the Oklahoma
dustbowl, traveled from coast to coast during the thirties and
blended overt protest songs with classic American folk music.
Traditional in form, Guthrie's songs often subtly reflected the
poverty-stricken "other America" he had personally experienced.
Yet, above all, Guthrie wrote songs of hope and change. Whether singing about poverty, the union struggle, or America's natural beauty, Guthrie's voice was affirmative. As Guthrie noted, he
"made up songs telling what [he] thought was wrong and how
to make it right, songs that said what everybody in the country
was thinking."⁹ Guthrie's optimism appropriately appears in the
title of his autobiography, *Bound for Glory*.

Shortly before World War II, Guthrie and a few rural-oriented
folk singers planted their traditional style in liberal, sophisticated
New York City. This cultural cross-fertilization eventually produced the hosts of urban writers who turned out the "message
songs" of our era and made the guitar a contemporary symbol of
social protest. Guthrie's New York activities also cemented the
urban folk song to the political Left. A good example of the radical drift was "The Almanac Singers," a group which included
Guthrie and Pete Seeger—a young Harvard dropout. The Alma-
nacs mixed traditional folk songs with leftist politics and were
especially enthusiastic about singing for labor unions. Characteristically, they recorded an album of antiwar songs but withdrew
it in 1941 when Germany turned on Russia. They then completed
a record urging American intervention in the war, and Guthrie
and Seeger joined the armed forces.¹⁰

⁹ Quoted in Donald Myers, *Ballads, Blues, and the Big Beat* (New
York: Macmillan Co., 1966), p. 45.

¹⁰ On the career of the Almanac Singers see Gordon Friesen, "The
Almanac Singers," *Broadside*, no. 8 (June, 1962); no. 9 (July, 1962);
and no. 15 (November, 1962).

After the war, these same urban folk singers tried to use music as a lever for social reform. In 1946 Seeger and others established a New York group called People's Songs, and they published a magazine of the same name. The periodical crusaded for civil rights, militant unionism, and peace with Russia—both editorially and through topical songs. Some ballads, like "Listen Mr. Bilbo," ridiculed such southern segregationists as Mississippi Senator Ted Bilbo. Another song, "The Gol-dern Red," lampooned union-busting, segregation, and red-baiting all in one package. Three verses of the latter ballad immediately sum up People's Songs' style and goals:[11]

The speed-up was terrific, and the pay was mighty small,
So we organized a union one fine day
I said "Boss you better talk, or we'll have to take a walk"
And here's the very words I heard him say—(and I quote)
    Why you're nothing but a gol-dern red (agitator)
    Why you're nothing but a gol-dern red.
    If you're for the CIO, you're a stooge for Uncle Joe

. . . .

    If you strike for higher wages, you've been reading Lenin's pages
    Yes, you're nothing but a gol-dern red.
I took a Negro brother out to get some hash with me.
The waitress blushed and looked the other way,
The owner said 'Get out—we don't want your kind about,
And you won't get served in here til Judgment Day' (Here it comes)
    Why you're nothing but a gol-dern red (just like Lincoln)
    Why you're nothing but a gol-dern red.
    If you think a man's a man when his skin is black or tan
    Then you're nothing but a gol-dern red.
Here's the moral to my story; if you strike for higher pay

11 *People's Songs Bulletin* 3 (February–March, 1948):3–4; copyright *Sing Out*, used by permission.

If discrimination gets you good and mad
If you get into a fight for insisting on our rights
Then you're sure to be denounced for something bad (Guess what)
　　Why you're nothing but a gol-dern red (Great God)
　　Why you're nothing but a gol-dern red.

Songs like this seem relatively mild today, but during the cold-war hysteria, People's Songs was immediately labeled ultraradical and pushed farther to the Left. The increasingly conservative and image-conscious union movement ignored People's Songs, while more militant groups, which welcomed any support, embraced it. In its brief three-year history it participated in enough left-wing rallies to ruin the reputation of a dozen organizations. People's Songs did not work directly with radicals, but its willingness to sing for such groups as the American Communist party, the American Labor party, and Henry Wallace's Progressive party made radicalism and folk singing almost synonymous. For example, a standard anti-Communist joke of the period described two Communist comrades organizing a meeting: :"You bring the Negro," says one. "I'll bring the folk singer."[12] Not surprisingly, People's Songs was investigated and harassed by the House Committee on Un-American Activities, and, characteristically, the group fought back with songs satirizing the Committee's work. Inevitably, in 1949, People's Songs folded, along with its badly beaten favorite candidate—Henry Wallace.[13]

The remnant of these protest writers went underground during the early 1950's, with anti-Communist groups snapping at their

[12] Quoted in Oscar Brand, *The Ballad Mongers* (New York: Funk and Wagnalls, 1962), p. 128.

[13] On the goals and aims of the People's Songs group, see R. Serge Denisoff, "Urban Folk 'Movement' Research: Value Free?" *Western Folklore* 28 (July, 1969):183–197; "The Proletarian Renascence: The Folkness of the Ideological Folk," *Journal of American Folklore* 82 (January, 1969):51–65.

heels. Counterattack, an organization committed to purging America's mass media of radicals in general and Communists in particular, had, since 1947, attempted to blacklist singers by publicizing their associations with alleged subversive groups. Counterattack was especially effective during the McCarthy era's red scare. Its newsletter, also named *Counterattack*, and its bible, a slim volume titled *Red Channels: The Report of Communist Influence in Radio and Television*, became standard reference works for media executives. Accordingly, even when folk music became popular in the 1960's, older performers like Pete Seeger continued to be blacklisted. In any event, protest songs did not re-enter the mass culture until the McCarthy influence had dissipated and Martin Luther King emerged as a leader in the civil rights movement.

People's Songs had completely failed to rally America into one great union through song, but it did produce scores of ballads that became models for the protest songs of the 1960's. Moreover, People's Songs symbolized the faith that solidarity and communication through music could generate social action. The optimism is still the most striking difference between the earlier protest writers and today's more cynical young artists. Close connection with the unions probably oversimplified the struggle for the older writers. Their solution was always to join ranks, sing, and coerce reform by the growing weight of numbers. Thus, in 1963, Theo Bikel appeared at a civil rights rally with many veteran singers and noted that they had come to signify their "conviction that not a single one of us will ever be free until we all are."[14] Similarly, in 1969, Pete Seeger reaffirmed his optimism by denying that politics was "the art of the possible." Rather, Seeger insisted, "the real art of politics is to make what appears to be im-

[14] Theodore Bikel, "They Are My People," *Liberation* 7 (October, 1963):5.

possible, possible."[15] This earlier optimism and solidarity would quickly break down during the complex sixties. The youth culture was not interested in organizing, but in freeing itself from organizational restraints. Increasingly, the writer-performers were neither optimistic nor pessimistic, but rather existential in their outlook. In an age of generation gaps, an obvious gulf developed between the earlier protest singers and their musical heirs. A primary cause was the tendency of younger writers to base their songs on secondary perceptions of society—usually from mass media. For older singers like Seeger, songs were weapons to be used in a struggle they had already joined. In contrast, younger protest singers tended simply to catalogue social ills without taking part in their cure.

These subtle changes in outlook evolved between 1955 and 1965—a period which saw a steady rise in the popularity of topical, radical music. Yet commercial success left its mark and completely changed protest music's form, goals, and style. In the late 1950's, numerous cultural changes encouraged the revival of folk music and eventually of protest songs. Earlier in the decade, a radical image had forced folk singers to concentrate on traditional American folk songs. However, protest songs were an important part of that tradition, and now, as part of the nation's heritage, they projected a more wholesome image. Imperceptibly, folk music captured college audiences by moving into a musical vacuum. While jazz had become increasingly hazy and complex, rock-and-roll had steadily become more nonsensical and meaningless. High school students, raised on rock, were ready for something more sophisticated when they entered college in the late 1950's, and folk music took over by default.

The nonviolent southern civil rights movement gave even greater impetus to protest music. From the start, the sit-in move-

[15] Pete Seeger's column in *Sing Out* 19 (December–January, 1969): 39.

ment was also a sing-in movement, as demonstrators wrote new songs and rewrote old ones to fit the occasion.[16] Sympathetic northern songwriters, like Bob Dylan and Phil Ochs, pitched in with musical polemics against discrimination, the arms race, and middle-class conformity. Gifted singers, like Judy Collins and Joan Baez, and polished liberal groups, like the Chad Mitchell Trio and Peter, Paul, and Mary, attracted an ever-growing audience. As the general folk craze continued, the protest characteristics of the movement were diluted, but protest songs still projected the most vivid picture of the folk revival. Thus, in 1961, *Newsweek* reported: "Basically the schools and students that support causes support folk music. Find a campus that breeds Freedom Riders, Anti-Birch demonstrators, and anti-bomb societies, and you'll find a folk group. The connection is not fortuitous."[17] The 1962 publication of *Broadside*, a magazine specializing in protest ballads, and the new radical editorial stress of *Sing Out*, an older folk periodical, also indicated protest music's rise. Political lyrics were suddenly a musical vogue. Songwriter Roger McGuinn recalled that, although he had never been particularly socially conscious, he found himself "trying to get a political message into almost everything" he wrote, simply because there was a "left-wing thing" in the air.[18]

By 1965 folk popularity had turned in a new direction. Commercial interests saw an opportunity to merge the high school and college markets by combining rock-and-roll with folk music.

[16] For a perceptive study of the relation between the civil rights movement and folk music, see Josh Dunson, *Freedom in the Air* (New York: International Publishers, 1965).

[17] *Newsweek*, November 27, 1961, p. 84.

[18] "Interview with Roger McGuinn of the Byrds," *Sing Out*, 18 (December, 1968):11. On the continuity and roles of *People's Songs*, *Broadside*, and *Sing Out*, see Dick Reuss, "Topical Songs from *People's Songs* to *Broadside*: The Changing Times," *Broadside*, no. 55 (February, 1965).

The result was folk-rock and the beginning of the psychedelic revolution. Electronic equipment steadily replaced folk guitars and brought "message" music to the best-seller charts. However, the amplified topical songs were usually too general to be meaningful and too loud to be intelligible. This was probably inevitable, for as topical music became commercial, it became profitable to protest electronically—something, or anything, or, best of all, everything. Folk-rock registered protest, but it was usually symbolic rather than substantive dissent. Just as Simon Kunen, a student radical, viewed his hair as a symbol of revolt, so might many a political radical say of psychedelic music: "But as for bad vibrations emanating from my follicles (or music) I say great. I want the cops to sneer and the old ladies swear and the businessmen worry. I want everyone to see me and say: 'There goes an enemy of the state' because that's where I'm at, as we say in the Revolution biz."[19]

Moreover, that was often the way it was in the protest business. Songs had to portray their anti-Establishment credentials with the right slogans and with a suitably loud volume, while the performer had to adopt an acceptably weird life style. Ric Masten's talking blues song, "The Protest Biz,"[20] makes the point succinctly:

Got a call the other day, got a buzz from Sodom
Down near Mickey Mouse land.
Man says: I hear ya got songs baby? Protest songs 'bout peace
    and labor strikes, freedom songs of civil rights.
An' I said: Yes it's true. An' he says: Cool, baby cool!
Says: I think you're a damn fool

[19] James Simon Kunen, *The Strawberry Statement* (New York: Harper and Row, 1969), p. 72.
[20] Ric Masten's "The Protest Biz," copyright 1967 by Mastensville Music Publishing (BMI), used by permission.

But I never let politics stand between me and money.
I'm gonna make us both a bundle sweetie!
I think you're a pink fink
But that's the way it is in the protest biz!
Said: I want ya to sign on the dotted line sweetie
I want ya to point your finger for me at thirty-three and a third.
I'll put your picture
All psychedelic and like that on the record jacket,
With your big guitar and your long hair hangin' down.
But I'm goin' bald, I said.
An' he said: Oh I'm sorry, I must have the wrong number.
But I got a beard, say I. Groovy! says he,
I think you're a damn red an' I wish you were dead
But like I said:
That's the way it is in the protest biz.
Are you interested? I said: No, I don't think so.
He said: Now don't blow your cool sweetheart!
Whatcha writin' them songs for?
Ya want to reach the people, dontcha?
Well come to me baby, if ya got a message,
Not Western Union.
Who do you think you're reachin' singin' to the walls like that?
Come to me baby and be heard.
I'll make ya rich and famous
Ya dirty Commie!
But that's the way it is in the protest biz.
Well I think it's a lousy way to make a buck, I said.
Now, don't point your finger at me babe!
Like where would you be without war and Watts
And poverty. Without labor strikes and tragedy,
You'd be out of business sweetie, with nothin' to sing about!
Beautiful, I said, I'll sing about faith, hope and charity.
It won't sell man! he said.
And I said: Mister . . .
And he said: Call me sweetheart!

So I said: Sweetheart. An' he said: Yeah?
And I said: Go to hell!
And he said: Well, that's the way it is in the protest biz.
And then he hung up.

Yet it is naive to pass off the influence of rock music by poking
fun at its commercial trappings—clothes, ridiculous group names,
and zany antics. The diverse, illogical, sensory nature of rock
music may be quite appropriate for youth in general and radical
youth in particular. As songwriter Malvina Reynolds suggested,
today's generation is "word sick." They have "been talked at, lec-
tured at," and commercially propagandized until "they believe
nothing and are influenced by everything."[21] Rock singer Country Joe McDonald indicated that really grasping the total reality
of Vietnam would probably drive him insane. Answering his own
question as to what you do about it, Country Joe replied: "You
take drugs, you turn up the music very loud, you dance around,
you build yourself a fantasy world where everything's beautiful."
However, McDonald's group, "Country Joe and the Fish," has
also mixed antiwar songs, like "Fixin to Die Rag," in with psychedelic escape music.[22] Thus, hard-rock sometimes meets the
absurdity of the world by overwhelming distasteful reality with
an existential world of personal emotion.

There is no direct link between psychedelic dropouts and political terrorists, yet both have discarded rational dialogue and
live in an alienated world which either completely rejects or completely embraces ideology. Thus it is not surprising that when the
"Rolling Stones," a British rock quartet, first came to the West
Coast, a small, violent splinter group issued a proclamation of
welcome which noted:

[21] Malvina Reynolds, Letter to the Editor, in *Broadside*, no. 83
(August, 1967), p. 7.
[22] "Country Joe Unstrung," *Sing Out* 18 (June, 1968): 20–21.

Greeting and welcome Rolling Stones, our comrades in the desperate battle against the maniacs who hold power. The Revolutionary youth of the world hears your music and is inspired to even more deadly acts. . . .

. . . .

We will play your music in rock-n-roll marching bands as we tear down the jails and free the prisoners, as we tear down the State schools and free the students. . . .[23]

The "Rolling Stones" are non-political and definitely uninterested in overthrowing capitalism. However, the "Stones" scorn rational discourse, and their song lyrics are hazy enough to be perceived as radical hymns. Thus their "Street Fighting Man," a best-selling record which said nothing about political upheaval, is often seen as a revolutionary marching song because of its title and fervor.

Yet, if the "Stones" are not opposed to capitalism, it is at least their business to appear anti-Establishment. Here is where radical activists and psychedelic dropouts come together at the bandstand or jukebox. Youthful alienation is primarily based on the belief that impersonal powers control one's life. There are two classic responses—either drop out or fight the machine.[24] Often both dropouts and activists see themselves as radical reformers. The activist seeks to change the world, while the dropout's dissent is a personal negation of society. The radical activist generally patronizes the dropout, but is willing to view rejection of society as a possible first step toward political action. Most younger radicals have given up on the American worker as a reform vehicle and have turned to a wider cultural approach which sees youth as

[23] Ralph J. Gleason, "Like a Rolling Stone," in Eisen, *The Age of Rock*, p. 72. Also see Alan Coren, "Head Stone," *Playboy*, November, 1969, pp. 162–164.

[24] For a brilliant study of culturally alienated youth see Kenneth Kenniston, *The Uncommitted* (New York: Dell Publishing Co., 1960).

a revolutionary class. Thus, radicals have increasingly adopted C.
Wright Mills's view that the new struggle is not between classes
but between the "power elite" and the masses. The power elite
control the media; hence the radical cultural effort strives to reach
the young before they can be programmed. Popular music is now
a major political weapon, since the new radicalism is primarily
a youth movement. The cliché, "don't trust anyone over thirty,"
is one tired example; but perhaps it is less clear that the prime
pacifist theme pervading psychedelic music, "make love not
war," is hardly directed at the older generation.[25]

Precisely because today's radical finds it so difficult to confront
his adversary in our complex corporate society, the new political
battleground is largely cultural and generational rather than social
and economic. This new struggle has recently been popularized as
"The Making of a Counter Culture."[26] The idea is to reject and
destroy the old culture in order to liberate the individual. While
some see this as a negative, destructive act, many radicals insist
that it is a positive move which forces critical evaluation of society.[27] In this regard, popular music can sometimes be a vehicle for
cultural fragmentation.

Ironically, music's vast power to influence was sensed by the
often ludicrous professional anti-Communist groups long before

[25] Bottomore, *Critics of Society*, p. 101.
[26] Theodore Roszak, *The Making of a Counter Culture* (New York:
Doubleday and Co., 1969); R. Serge Denisoff and Mark H. Levine,
"Mannheim's Problem of Generations and Counter Culture: A Study
in the Ideology of Music" (paper presented at the 1970 Pacific Sociological Association Annual Meeting). Also, for a perceptive critique
of Roszak's work, see Michael Lerner, "Anarchism and the American
Counter Culture," *Government and Opposition* 5 (Autumn, 1970):
430–455.
[27] Note that a radical group at Indiana University has published a
"disorientation booklet," for freshmen, to compete with the official
orientation pamphlet.

the issue of a counter culture arose. For example, in 1965, Rev. David Noebel, of the fiercely Fundamentalist and anti-Communist Christian Crusade in Tulsa, Oklahoma, sounded the alarm. In two amazing books, *Communism, Hypnotism, and the Beatles* and *Rhythm, Riots, and Revolution,* the Reverend Mr. Noebel thoroughly accepted Pete Seeger's comment that "the guitar could be mightier than the bomb."[28] Noebel concluded that Communists had infiltrated and subverted American folk-and-rock music to hypnotically brainwash American youth with Marxist ideology. As far as Noebel was concerned "the noise" that millions of young people called music was "invigorating, vulgarizing, and orgiastic." While destroying youth's "ability to relax, reflect, study, and meditate," it in fact prepared them "for riot, civil disobedience, and revolution." Thus, Noebel viewed the marriage of rock and folk music as "a total capitulation on the part of U. S. record companies to the Red-infested folk field."[29] He warned that this synthesis "could well spell the doom" of America, since no nation could "long endure with its younger generation singing itself into defeatism, pessimism, a peace-at-any-price mentality, disarmament, appeasement, surrender, fear of death, hatred toward the South, atheism, immorality and negation of patriotism." For Noebel, the effectiveness of the "Marxist folksingers" in making their listeners "feel nauseated at living in America" was illustrated by the "togetherness of . . . folksingers and student rioters" and also by teenagers "screaming in Beatle concerts."[30] In 1965 Noebel's work seemed typical of the Communist-conspiracy syndrome. However, today, in the midst

[28] David Noebel, *Communism, Hypnotism, and the Beatles* (Tulsa: Christian Crusade Publications, 1965); *Rhythm, Riots, and Revolution* (Tulsa: Christian Crusade Publications, 1966).

[29] Noebel, *Rhythm, Riots, and Revolution,* pp. 21, 146.

[30] Ibid., pp. 176, 196, 212.

of a cultural war for the allegiance of the young, Noebel's analysis seems somewhat less ludicrous, once divorced from the paranoid issue of Communist subversion.

Much psychedelic music does project a hypnotic mood rather than a message. In effect, it says: "Don't listen to what I say, watch what I do, or, more accurately, the way I do it." Though the lyrics are not explicit, the music exerts an indirect radical influence by showing contempt for social mores in such areas as sexual behavior, obscenity, and drug use. Also, since cultural changes are often more shocking than calls for fundamental social reform, radical political positions may look harmless by comparison. Drug songs, for example, are often more distasteful to the radio audience than political songs and have recently become a public issue. In December, 1969, television personality Art Linkletter asserted that half of the most popular records were "concerned with secret messages to teenagers to drop out, turn on, and groove with chemicals." And in September, 1970, Vice-President Agnew charged that much of "rock music glorifies drug usage."[31] Indeed, many radio stations have long banned overt drug songs, but they have often overlooked the lyrical double meanings of such songs as Bob Dylan's hazy, mystic "Mr. Tambourine Man," and John Lennon's "Lucy in the Sky with Diamonds." It is natural for drugs to be a topic of rock music, since the songs reflect the world of youth and young singers. Whether or not the young take them, drugs are a definite part of their culture, just as alcohol is an important ingredient of the adult world. Thus, drinking is commonly mentioned in the lyrics of dozens of songs popularized by earlier generations. However,

[31] *The New York Times*, September 15, 1970. Linkletter made his comment October 24, 1969, before the House Select Committee on Illegal Drugs, after the drug-induced death of his daughter (UPI story in the *Fort Worth Press*, December 7, 1969, p. 21).

those who insist that psychedelic music has a specific cultural or political message are deluded. Its major quality is an existential stress. Folk-rock influences by rejecting social control and by allowing one to read almost anything into the lyrics. The music represents a life style, and while it may help induce political radicalism, it destroys specific political protest. By saying everything, it must in effect say nothing.[32]

One writer divides classic protest songs logically into magnetic and rhetorical types. While the magnetic songs aimed at building group solidarity and adding members to the movement, the rhetorical sought to pinpoint specific conditions that called for redress.[33] But folk-rock songs fit in neither category. They call not for solidarity, but for diversity; they do not point out specific social ills, they depict general absurdity. The older protest songs made radicals feel better, but they usually did not make many converts—the listeners were convinced in advance. Popular music with a vague protest theme can make some converts subtly. Youths first attracted by the music may later imbibe the style and finally perhaps read something of personal significance into the lyrics. Even serious Establishment organizations now often try to get their ideas across through rock music. Thus, the Campus Crusade for Christ sends a folk-rock group called "Armageddon" from campus to campus in an avowed effort "to change the world." The advertising flyer they distribute to students jauntily announces that Armageddon has "a sound that competes with

[32] A good selection of rock lyrics is contained in *Rock Is Beautiful: An Anthology of American Lyrics*, edited by Stephanie Spinner (New York: Dell Publishing Co., 1970).

[33] R. Serge Denisoff, "Songs of Persuasion: A Sociological Analysis of Urban Propaganda Songs," *Journal of American Folklore* 79 (October–December, 1966): 581–588; "Protest Movements: Class Consciousness and the Propaganda Song," *Sociological Quarterly* 9 (1968): 228–247.

the top in pop and a message that tops the top. . . . Judge for yourself. Allow Armageddon's electrical sound to massage your ears and rap with your mind."[34]

From religious appeals (including folk masses) to commercial and even political advertising, music as communication is everywhere triumphant. The question is not its use, but its immediate and long-term effects, especially on the coming generation. Mankind has a long sad history of noticing the revolutionary effects of new technology too late. We still know little about what happens to a generation brought up on television or even about the social effects of the telephone. We know less about the influence of message songs. Some suggest that song lyrics may have a subliminal effect and act as a catalyst for alienation or political action. Others insist that protest songs usually serve as a symbolic substitute for personal involvement. After all, it is only too easy to feel that you are moving society when all you are doing is listening to records, or singing along.

Yet, if the new popular music does not induce overt radical action, it can produce a new kind of togetherness that borders on the hypnotic. Singing in a group or listening alone, one feels bold. Thoreau noted: "When I hear music, I fear no danger. I am invulnerable. I see no foe. I am related to the earliest times, and to the latest."[35] Similarly, singing protest marchers are often charged with a communal euphoria, which can constitute the emotional highlight of their dissent. For example, in 1969, a University of Wisconsin coed criticized *Newsweek* magazine for concentrating on the few violent incidents in a campus demonstration, while ignoring "the 10,000 peaceful marchers singing

[34] Handbill distributed at The University of Texas at Arlington, February 18, 1970.

[35] On the religious fervor of protest songs, see Jerome L. Rodnitzky, "The New Revivalism," *South Atlantic Quarterly* 70 (Spring, 1971): 13–21.

together by torchlight."[36] By torchlight, by daylight, on the march, or in the concert hall, there is a magic that can be sensed if not rationalized. Perhaps the charisma comes across best in the key line of the Paul McCartney–John Lennon song, "The Word": "Say the word and be like me. Say the word and you'll be free." The word was, of course, *love,* but at a given rally the magic word might be *freedom,* or *peace.*[37]

However, increasingly, charisma, hypnotism, and euphoria are big business and, in terms of the youth market, very profitable. This does not alarm some reformers. For example, Simon Kunen, the young radical writer, feels that capitalism has "a self destruct mechanism." Kunen argues that the corporate media only seek profit, and if radical, revolutionary materials are profitable, corporations will disseminate radicalism and revolution.[38] Most radicals are far more pessimistic and feel that the mass media co-opt radicalism by diluting its content and dulling its fervor. For example, when protest songs are accompanied by a full orchestra, art is improved but the message and ardor suffer. Likewise, when President Lyndon Johnson proclaimed "We Shall Overcome," the song and slogan lost much of its meaning. And while the pacifist ballad "Universal Soldier" became a nationwide hit, the Vietnamese War accelerated. More ironically, Glen Campbell, who recorded "Universal Soldier," supported the war and was quoted as saying that "anyone who wouldn't fight for his country was no real man."[39] Hence, many radicals have re-

[36] Letter to *Newsweek* editor from Sue Griffin, printed in *Newsweek,* March 17, 1969.

[37] See John Lennon and Paul McCartney's "The Word," reproduced in *Journey to Freedom,* edited by Landon Gerald Downey (Chicago: The Swallow Press, 1969), p. 30.

[38] Kunen, quoted from an interview on the CBS television show, "Camera Three," July 12, 1970. Frank Zappa expresses a similar view in Kofsky, "Frank Zappa Interview," p. 257.

[39] Tom Paxton quoted Glen Campbell in "An Interview with Tom

jected commercial music as a reform vehicle. Irwin Silber, former editor of *Sing Out*, recently concluded that popular music's "cultural revolution" is a threat to radical reform. He argued that the American working class "instinctually senses" that electronic folk-rock "is basically a middle class trip." Although Silber believed the youthful alienation the new music reflects is a chief symptom of capitalist society's disintegration, he also felt that doing your own thing is a "bourgeoisie trait" on which capitalism is based. Silber charged that "groovy life styles" suggest that workers ignore the system that oppresses them rather than fight to change it.[40]

At the same time, since music is only a tool, songs may become a conservative or even racist force. The Left has perpetuated the myth that protest songs are by definition humanitarian attacks against the status quo. Historically, this has not always been the case. For example, the Ku Klux Klan used songs to further their movement. The words of "The Klansman's Jubilee," sung to the tune of "The Battle Hymn of the Republic" were "We rally 'round Old Glory in our robes of spotless white;/While the fiery cross is burning, in the silent silv'ry night/Come join our glorious army in the cause of God and Right,/The Klan is marching on. . . ."[41]

Another example is a 1961 song parody called "Kosher Christ-

———

Paxton," *Broadside*, no. 67 (February, 1966), p. 8. Tom Paxton, "Folk Rot," *Sing Out* 15 (January, 1966): 103. Paxton noted that although rock versions of Bob Dylan's integrationist ballad, "Blowin' in the Wind," were danced to in many a "lily-white" southern fraternity house, there was "no rush to sign up Negro brothers."

[40] Irwin Silber, "The Cultural Retreat," *Guardian*, December 6, 1969, p. 17. Also see Irwin Silber, "Fan the Flames," *Sing Out* 18 (March, 1968): 39.

[41] Emerson Hunsberger Loucks, *Ku Klux Klan in Pennsylvania: A Study in Nativism* (New York: The Telegraph Press, 1936), p. 122. See also Marcello Truzzi, "Folksongs on the Right," *Sing Out* 13 (October, 1963): 51, 53.

mas," which was published in *Thunderbolt,* the periodical of the
National States' Rights party. In part, the lyrics proclaimed:

> Out of the East came three wise men,
> Levy, Goldberg, and Uncle Ben
> The Christians all spend for Xmas Day
> And Goldberg will give six months to pay
>
> . . . .
>
> Down the chimney old Santa comes
> With a bag of toys from Isaac Blums
> Ring out the old, Ring in the new
> While your money goes to some foxy Jew. [42]

The downtrodden poor may agree with Havelock Ellis that
"if a man cannot sing as he carries his cross he had better drop
it," but conservatives are more likely to paraphrase the revivalist
and ask: "Why should the [radicals] have all the good tunes?"
Indeed, the recent success of conservative and patriotic country-
and-western songs, like Merle Haggard's "The Fightin' Side of
Me" and "Okie from Muskogee," as well as Guy Drake's "Welfare Cadillac," suggests that protest songs on the Right may become a permanent feature of popular music and that records may
become an ideological battleground.[43]

Commercialism may destroy music's political influence by sub-
verting the performer as well as by diluting the content. Many
former protest singers have cut topical songs from their repertory,
either to increase their earnings, or because they tired of preach-
ing. For example, in 1969 singer Judy Collins stated that she no
longer wished to "be a political agitator." She decided that protest songs were merely "finger pointing," dividing people, where-

[42] Song, "Kosher Christmas," reproduced in letter, *Sing Out* 12 (April,
1962): 59.

[43] On this point see R. Serge Denisoff, "Kent State, Muskogee, and
the White House," *Broadside,* no. 108 (July, 1970) pp. 2–4.

as she felt music should unite them. [44] Similarly, Woody Guthrie's son, Arlo, whose song, "Alice's Restaurant," registered a devastating attack on the military draft, said he felt that "you don't accomplish very much singing protest songs to people who agree with you. Everybody just has a good time thinking they're right." [45] Furthermore, most successful younger songwriters, like Leonard Cohen, Joni Mitchell, and Tim Harden, forsake social subjects for deeply personal themes written in abstract poetic form.

Thus Gordon Friesen, editor of *Broadside,* recently complained that, although a variety of good protest material is being written, recording companies refuse to feature it. Friesen felt that many folk singers sold out by singing "meaningless fluff about . . . clouds, flowers, butterflies . . . Suzannes . . . and the like." [46] Indeed, some former topical singers even avoid calling themselves folk singers and describe themselves as singers of "contemporary art songs."

The trend away from topical songs was started by Bob Dylan, the most creative and influential writer-performer of the past decade. Dylan had started out to emulate Woody Guthrie, and his early, overt protest songs, "Blowin' in the Wind," "Masters of War," and "The Times They Are A-Changin'," earned him the adoration of the political left. Dylan, however, felt his creativity had become captive to ideology, and in 1965 he declared his independence. Thereafter, his songs were intensely personal, hazy statements, with electronically amplified musical arrangements. He made his new philosophy crystal clear in a remarkable song titled, "My Back Pages." In this ballad Dylan proclaimed that he had oversimplified right and wrong in his earlier songs

---

[44] "An Interview with Judy Collins," *Life*, May 2, 1969, pp. 45–46.

[45] Arlo Guthrie, quoted in "Woody's Boy," *Newsweek*, May 23, 1966, p. 110.

[46] Editorial, *Broadside*, no. 107 (June, 1970), pp. 9–10.

and had become what he most hated—a preacher. One line noted that he had deluded himself into believing that "liberty was just equality in school." However, at the end of each verse, Dylan explained that he was "much older then," but "younger than that now."[47] After "My Back Pages," protest music in general became younger, less ideological, and much vaguer in its content and influence.

Yet direct, serious protest songs are far from obsolete. They will probably never attain the commercial popularity they enjoyed in the early 1960's, but they remain a powerful American art form. Protest ballads still play a central role in America's major contemporary social struggles. The continued publication of *Broadside* magazine, the dozens of antipollution and pacifist songs, and the recent recording of a protest-song album by the Black Panther party are ample evidence that musical ballads will continue to be a radical political force in the 1970's.[48] However, even when songs are used by very militant groups, they will likely remain peculiarly American. For example, at a 1967 symposium in Cuba, Xuan Hong, a Vietcong singer, defined a protest song as "militant in content, national in form and popular in idiom."[49] These criteria have little relation to American protest songs. Our most effective protest ballads have been subtle rather than militant, poetic rather than merely idiomatic, and their orientation has been universal rather than nationalistic. American protest music has invariably sought to make individuals feel guilty. As

[47] Bob Dylan, "My Back Pages," in *Another Side of Bob Dylan*, Columbia Record album, 1965.

[48] The Black Panther album, *Seize the Time*, was offered for sale by their "Ministry of Education" in an advertisement in *Broadside*, no. 107 (June, 1970). For an example of leading songs against the Vietnam War, see Barbara Dane and Irwin Silber, eds., *The Vietnam Songbook* (New York: Guardian Press, 1969).

[49] Transcript of symposium on protest songs in Havana, Cuba, *Sing Out* 17 (October, 1967): 30.

songwriter Buffy St. Marie noted, many Americans grow up believing that social problems are someone else's fault, and topical songs can dramatically suggest personal responsibility for social ills.[50]

The really serious protest singers have usually been on the fringes of mass culture, but their influence cannot be measured statistically. The small audiences they garnered were often activists who stimulated many others. Also, radical songwriters subtly influenced more popular fellow artists through artful, topical lyrics and their own personal moral commitment. The medium may, as Marshall McLuhan insists, be the message, but this should not obscure the importance of messages within a medium. In our multimedia culture there is a multiplier effect. Other media, especially films and television, reinforce specific ideas that songs suggest. Films like M*A*S*H and Catch-22 reinforce pacifist songs, and the graphic television coverage of the Vietnam War and the resistance to it stimulates both pacifism and the act of dissent.

The generational results are striking. In the 1950's relatively few college students were radicalized during their college years. Generally, not until they were juniors and seniors did they suspect that American society had serious faults. However, in the late 1960's, relatively large numbers of freshmen entered the universities already dissatisfied with American society. As early as 1964 James Dennison, a Michigan State University administrator, complained: "These kids today are so darned serious they worry us."[51] Popular protest music has played an integral part

---

[50] Buffy St. Marie, on CBS television show "Camera Three," August 30, 1970.

[51] "Changes in Today's College Students," U.S. News and World Report, February 17, 1964, p. 67.

in making numbers of youth more serious, radical, and politically worrisome.

Yet, increasingly, protest music's influence becomes broader and harder to pinpoint. Young radicals and youth in general consistently stress the desirability of personal choice and diversity. The goal is to renounce doctrine and exhibit a personal moral commitment. Thus folk writer-performers have often become models for activist youth. Traditionally, the folk singer was a brawny Negro laborer, a white ex-convict, or perhaps an Ivy League-educated folklorist. Today's folk singer, however, is more likely to be an alienated college dropout, seeking self-identity through his own music. Moreover, many singers symbolize personal integrity. Young radicals feel that Joan Baez, Tom Paxton, or Bob Dylan cannot be bought, in the traditional show-business sense. Thus, even though Bob Dylan has given up explicit message songs, he remains popular with radical youth, because he consistently functions as a social rebel and refuses to bow to the press, or to the fans, or to musical fads. Many preach doing your own thing, but Dylan lives it. Thus he remains a credible existential hero and a radical cultural symbol.

In an era pervaded by fear of youthful dissent, contemporary observers are unlikely to assess the radical influence of popular music with any degree of detachment. Yet the pace of change is too rapid to wait until the dust settles and passions cool. Historians are well aware that outlandish past radicalisms have often become the fashionable reforms of the present—that what was too much in one decade can be too little in the next. What present-day cultural radicals loosely call "the movement," seems to some childish nonsense, to others a devilish conspiracy to destroy America, while to many of the radicals themselves it constitutes a holy crusade. In any case, it is clear that many youths are seeking something our society does not supply, and to some extent various forms of popular protest music fulfill their needs.

In 1968 social critic Paul Goodman lamented that America had no credible program of social reconstruction and sadly noted: "The young are honorable and see the problems, but they don't know anything because we have not taught them anything."[52] The same year Country Joe McDonald sensed "an incredible amount of energy coming out of the young kids" from the "black ghetto . . . and a white hippie ghetto." He suggested that these forces were lying dormant and asserted: "If someone can come along and tell them which way to go or what to do, then I'd say maybe we got a revolution."[53]

However, Country Joe never said what kind of revolution; and our protest music provides neither direction nor leadership. Songs, after all, "lie only halfway between thought and action" and unfortunately "may become a substitute for both."[54] Yet many of our affluent young people probably embrace protest songs because they lend meaning to their otherwise aimless, amoral lives and because the songs salve their guilt and proclaim their humanity and their fellowship with the oppressed. If you consider our finest protest ballads both poetry and art, then perhaps it was John F. Kennedy who best explained their true influence and value, when he observed: "When power corrupts, poetry cleanses. For art establishes the basic human truth which must serve as the touchstone of our judgment. The highest duty of the writer, the composer, the artist is to remain true to himself, and let the chips fall where they may."[55]

Our best protest songs have indeed been a cleansing force. The songwriters have had the revivalist's faith that to hear of

[52] Paul Goodman, *The New York Times Magazine*, February 25, 1968, p. 6.

[53] "Country Joe Unstrung," p. 19.

[54] Pete Seeger, in his column in *Sing Out* 18 (June, 1968): 85.

[55] John F. Kennedy, quoted, in *Sing Out* 16 (February, 1966): 80.

evil is to hate it. Their songs constitute a radical influence, but, more importantly, they supply examples of conscience and principle to a society which has increasingly been unable to provide its youth with credible examples of either conscience or principle.

HARRY S. TRUMAN AND HIS CRITICS

The 1948 Progressives and the Origins of the Cold War

▭▭▭▭▭▭▭▭▭▭▭▭▭▭▭▭▭▭▭▭▭▭▭▭▭▭▭▭▭

BY FRANK ROSS PETERSON

IN 1922 WALTER LIPPMANN WROTE regarding public opinion: "There is the world outside and there are the pictures in our heads. Man behaves not according to the world as it really is but to the world as he thinks it is."[1] Thomas Bailey, the historian, added: "The truth is often less important than what people think is the truth."[2] For twenty-five years most Americans have had a vivid picture in their heads in which they fervently believe. It is a simple, ugly caricature depicting a quarter century of cold war. On one side are arrayed the forces of good: the United States and friends. Opposite this so-called free world are the forces of evil: a monolithic, aggressive Communist bloc. The conclusions are obvious. The free world, after defeating the supermilitaristic Axis powers, was forced to rearm in order to

[1] Walter Lippmann, *Public Opinion* (New York: Harcourt, Brace, 1922), p. 26.
[2] Thomas A. Bailey, *America Faces Russia* (Ithaca, N.Y.: Cornell University Press, 1964), p. vi.

contain a new satanic evil, Communist Russia, and, in the process, to save the world.[3] The picture is clear and concise, but is it completely true?

True or not, it is believed to be true, and Harry S. Truman's response to the threat of Soviet aggression has elevated him to high rungs on the presidential rating ladder. Never overly popular as Chief Executive, he has scored well with historians. The late Clinton Rossiter, a devoted student of the American presidency, reluctantly admitted that Truman will eventually win a place as a "near-great" president. He based his judgment on Truman administration programs designed to provide collective security against Communist expansion—such programs as the Truman Doctrine, the Marshall Plan, NATO, Point Four, and the Korean "police action."[4] A recent national survey of 571 American historians, conducted by sociologist Gary Maranell, revealed that Truman ranked in the top seven presidents, measured by the indices of prestige, strength of action, activeness, and accomplishments, and near the center of the spectrum

[3] Robert H. Ferrell, *American Diplomacy* (New York: W. W. Norton, 1969); Thomas A. Bailey, *A Diplomatic History of the American People* (New York: Appleton, Century, Crofts, 1969); Samuel F. Bemis, *A Diplomatic History of the United States* (New York: Holt, Rinehart & Winston, 1964), and Wayne Cole, *An Interpretive History of American Foreign Relations* (Homewood, Illinois: Dorsey Press, 1968) are considered to be standard texts. Three smaller monographs are Dexter Perkins, *The Diplomacy of a New Age* (Bloomington: Indiana University Press, 1967); John W. Spanier, *American Foreign Policy since World War II* (New York: Praeger, 1968); Robert Divine, ed., *American Foreign Policy since 1945* (Chicago: Quadrangle, 1969). Two excellent articles which state this view of the cold war are Arthur M. Schlesinger, Jr., "Origins of the Cold War," *Foreign Affairs* 46 (October, 1967): 22–52, and Norman A. Graebner, "Global Containment: The Truman Years," *Current History* 57 (August, 1969): 77–83, 115–116.

[4] Clinton Rossiter, *The American Presidency* (New York: Harcourt, Brace & World, 1960), pp. 158–159.

as to practicality, idealism, and flexibility.[5] His stature had substantially increased since 1962. This is the same man who left the White House in 1953 partially discredited. Republicans were shouting about corruption in the federal agencies; vast China had fallen prey to communism; the Soviet Union had detonated an atomic bomb; the nation's armed forces were stalemated in Korea; and Senator Joseph McCarthy was nipping at Truman's heels bellowing "soft on Communism."[6]

By the summer of 1946 two main currents of political unrest plagued Truman. One, articulated by Henry A. Wallace, was virulent criticism of his foreign policies—those same foreign policies which would vindicate him in historians' eyes two decades later. These historically significant attacks came, not from the right, but from liberal Democrats who, claiming to be true internationalists, believed that Truman's harsh cold war policies had precipitated global bipolarization. The other current of political unrest was evident in criticism of his domestic policies, particularly by labor leaders upset by his treatment of the railway unions and the United Mine Workers. Truman threatened to draft the railworkers if they struck, and he took over the mines and operated them in the name of the government when the mineworkers' strike threatened the nation with a fuel shortage. The labor leaders began to think in terms of a new, powerful labor party. Wallace originally wanted to operate within the Democratic party, but after his dismissal from Truman's cabinet

[5] Gary M. Maranell, "The Evaluation of the Presidents: An Extension of the Schlesinger Polls," *Journal of American History* 57 (June, 1970): 104–113. Arthur M. Schlesinger, Jr., conducted polls in 1948 and again in 1962.

[6] Eric Goldman, *The Crucial Decade and After, 1945–60* (New York: Random House, 1960), pp. 146–201. See also Cabell Phillips, *The Truman Presidency* (New York: Macmillan Co., 1962), pp. 253–432, and Richard H. Rovere, *Senator Joe McCarthy* (Cleveland: World Publishing Co., 1965).

he began to court the third-party advocates. Critics of Truman's domestic and foreign policies rallied around Wallace to form the 1948 Progressive party.[7]

Henry Wallace, a mystical idealist, was convinced that his years as secretary of agriculture, vice-president of the United States, and secretary of commerce had given him the experience needed to keep the nation from plunging into a disastrous atomic war. Considering himself the heir of Franklin D. Roosevelt's liberal policies, and believing that Truman had betrayed those policies, he openly criticized Truman while still in the cabinet. Truman, threatened with the resignation of Secretary of State Byrnes if Wallace was not silenced, axed Wallace, who then gravitated toward the ideologically like-minded.[8]

Another vociferous critic of Truman's foreign policy was Idaho's Senator Glen H. Taylor, a Democrat, former vaudeville actor and country-western singer, who thought that cooperation with the Soviet Union, rather than obvious and complete distrust, would move the world toward meaningful peace. Wallace and Taylor held such similar views on the origins of the cold war that eventually the two disenchanted New Dealers were drawn together.[9]

[7] David Shannon, *The Decline of American Communism* (New York: Harcourt, Brace & World, 1959), pp. 145–146, and Curtis D. MacDougall, *Gideon's Army*, 3 vols. (New York: Marzani and Munsell, 1965), I, 188–223. For a brief account of the labor disputes see Phillips, *The Truman Presidency*, pp. 113–119.

[8] Harry S. Truman, *Memoirs*, 2 vols. (New York: Doubleday and Co., 1956), I, 615. See Arthur H. Vandenberg, Jr., and J. A. Morris, eds., *The Private Papers of Senator Vandenberg* (Boston: Houghton Mifflin Co., 1952), pp. 300–302, and James F. Byrnes, *Speaking Frankly* (New York: Harper and Brothers, 1947), pp. 239–243.

[9] Karl M. Schmidt, *Henry A. Wallace: Quixotic Crusade* (Syracuse: Syracuse University Press, 1960), pp. 25–40. See also MacDougall, *Gideon's Army*, II, 307–310. For a complete analysis of Taylor's career, see F. Ross Peterson, "Liberal from Idaho: The Public Career of Glen H. Taylor" (Ph.D. dissertation, Washington State University, 1968).

Truman's containment philosophy, dramatically enunciated to
a joint session of Congress on March 12, 1947, provided the
nascency of the Progressive party. Truman told the Congress that
Communist guerrilla forces, operating from the surrounding
totalitarian states of Albania, Yugoslavia, and Bulgaria, threatened the overthrow of the Greek government. He reminded Congress that the United States and Great Britain shared a mutual
responsibility to preserve the political integrity of Greece and
Turkey, but that the British Empire was collapsing and was
going to pull out of Greece and Turkey on March 31.

The President said that the situation demanded immediate attention, and that the United Nations was in no position to assist.
Stating his belief that both military and economic aid were
necessary to prevent a Communist victory, Truman requested
$400 million immediately to shore up the tottering Greek and
Turkish regimes. Most of Truman's speech dealt with the situation in Greece, although he indicated that Turkey also needed
economic assistance. "The free peoples of the world look to us
for support in maintaining their freedoms," Truman declared.[10]
His plea was soon tabbed the "Truman Doctrine."

[10] U.S., Congress, *Congressional Record*, 80th Cong., 1st sess., 1947,
93, pt. 2: 1980–1981. For personal reflections on, as well as scholarly
analysis of, the Truman Doctrine and the philosophy of containment,
the following works proved especially helpful: George F. Kennan,
Memoirs (Boston: Little, Brown and Co., 1967), pp. 373–387; Dean
Acheson, *Present at the Creation* (New York: W. W. Norton and Co.,
1969), pp. 220–225; Walter Millis, ed., *The Forrestal Diaries* (New
York: Viking Press, 1951), pp. 210, 253–254; D. F. Fleming, *The
Cold War and Its Origins*, 2 vols. (New York: Doubleday and Co.,
1961), I, 443–476; Walter Lippmann, *The Cold War: A Study in U.S.
Foreign Policy* (New York: Harper and Brothers, 1947); Walter La-
Feber, *America, Russia, and the Cold War, 1945–1966* (New York:
John Wiley and Sons, 1967), pp. 37–65; William A. Williams, *The
Tragedy of American Diplomacy* (New York: Dell Publishing Co.,
1962), pp. 370–376; Ronald Steel, *Pax Americana* (New York: Viking
Press, 1967), pp. 15–27; David Horowitz, *The Free World Colossus*

Administration officials knew that there would be stiff opposition to the Truman Doctrine, and their expectations were
fulfilled. Glen Taylor told Acting Secretary of State Dean
Acheson that King Paul of Greece represented only a small
number of remaining monarchists and should be removed from
the throne as a precondition to American aid. He suggested
formation of a government "truly representative of all the democratic elements in Greece."[11] In Taylor's opinion, it would be
great to help people maintain their freedom if there was freedom to maintain. Viewing the administration's attempt to aid
Greece and Turkey in the name of anti-communism as an effort
to create unanimity by fear, he declared his willingness to help
democratic governments stay in power, but bitterly attacked
Greece and Turkey as anything but democratic, scoring the State
Department and the Truman Doctrine as well: "The gallant
warriors of the State Department, with their well-polished at-
taché cases bravely borne by well-manicured fingers, came riding
down the caucus room like the gallant 300 who held the pass
at Thermopylae. But the anti-communist guise hardly fits either,
for the Greek government bears no relationship whatever to
democracy, and it is not combatting communism."[12]

Henry Wallace's view of the Truman Doctrine was very grim.
On March 13, the day after Truman spoke, Wallace asserted to
a radio audience: "March 12, 1947, marked a turning point in
American history. It is not a Greek crisis we face, it is an Ameri-
can crisis. It is a crisis in the American spirit." Fearing that
Truman was in effect proposing that America police Russia's

(New York: Hill and Wang, 1965), pp. 69–96. The Fleming, Lippmann, LaFeber, Williams, Steel, and Horowitz accounts basically agree
with the Taylor-Wallace contemporary assessment of the Truman
Doctrine.

[11] *Salt Lake Tribune*, March 11, 1947.

[12] *Cong. Rec.*, 80th Cong., 1st sess., 1947, 93, pt. 3:2868.

every border, Wallace concluded that no nation was too reactionary for United States support provided it was near a Communist country, and further, "there is no country too remote to serve as the scene of a contest which may widen until it becomes a world war."

Although they had yet to form their coalition, Glen Taylor and Henry Wallace were in agreement. When Wallace contended that "when Truman offers unconditional aid to King Paul of Greece he is acting as the best salesman communism ever had,"[13] Taylor added, "for every Greek who was converted to communism by Russian propaganda last week, 100 have been converted by . . . the present Greek regime, and by our State Department's insistence that the only alternative to that regime is communism."[14]

Unable to meet the requested March 31 deadline, Congress continued to debate the Truman Doctrine until late in April. Taylor was in part responsible for this delay. Maintaining that all of the talk about a Communist takeover was merely a fog-bank blanketing the real economic issues, he again referred to the rich oil deposits of the Middle East and the fact that Britain's once powerful colonial empire was crumbling under the pressures of nationalism. He viewed the alleged Communist threat in Greece as minimal and in Turkey as nonexistent. He said: "We are told that the 13,000 Greek guerrillas will sweep down on Athens; and the 120,000 men of . . . King Paul aided by 10,000 British troops and equipped with the latest British arms will be helpless before them. We are told that the 13,000 will defeat the 130,000, and will establish a Communist dictatorship in Greece—even though it is admitted that most of the

[13] *New York Times*, March 14, 1947, p. 7. See MacDougall, *Gideon's Army*, I, 128–130, for a complete discussion of Wallace's reaction.

[14] *Cong. Rec.*, 80th Cong., 1st sess., 1947, 93, pt. 3:2868.

13,000 guerrillas are not Communist."[15] The Idaho lawmaker summarized his opposition to the Truman Doctrine when he declared that the United States was being asked to "underwrite backward regimes, intervene in civil war, and jeopardize the peace of the world—mainly on the basis of hints and innuendos, broad generalizations, and half-truths."[16]

Wallace, Taylor, and others opposed the Truman Doctrine initially because they believed that the United Nations should administer economic relief and that unilateral action on the part of the United States would cripple the effectiveness of the infant international organization. Agreeing that Greece needed economic aid, as did the people of many other war-devastated nations, Wallace asked, "If aid to the people of the world is our objective, why did the President and Congress allow the United Nations Relief and Reconstruction [Rehabilitation] Administration to die?"[17] Taylor and Senator Claude Pepper of Florida introduced a resolution which would provide money for Greece, but the money would be given directly to the United Nations for administration. Senator Arthur H. Vandenberg, chairman of the Senate Foreign Relations Committee, also criticized bypassing the United Nations. During the spring and summer of 1947, the United States did try to work with the United Nations in the Greek crisis, but the attempt was unsuccessful.[18]

While Congress continued debating the Truman Doctrine,

15 Ibid., p. 3387.

16 Ibid., p. 3388.

17 *New York Times*, March 14, 1947, p. 7. The United States used its financial veto power to terminate UNRRA and, in 1952, the International Refugee Organization. See Inis Claude, Jr., *Swords into Plowshares* (New York: Random House, 1956), p. 298, and Ferrell, *American Diplomacy*, pp. 692–694.

18 *Cong. Rec.*, 80th Cong., 1st sess., 1947, 93, pt. 2:2869. See also Cyril E. Black, "Greece and the United Nations," *Political Science Quarterly* 63 (December, 1948): 551–568.

Wallace left for Europe to review conditions firsthand. Leadership in the opposition to the Truman Doctrine then passed to Senator Taylor. Day after day Taylor pounded at the Truman proposal. Claiming that the program aimed at aiding Greece and Turkey involved an "oil-grab in the Middle East," Taylor concluded by saying that the objective of the Truman Doctrine was not so much "food for the Greek people as oil for the American monopolies—the oil that lies in the great lands just east of Greece and Turkey."[19]

Wallace and Taylor feared that the Truman Doctrine would further divide the world into two ideological camps. According to Taylor, if the United States pursued the pattern set by the Truman Doctrine proposal, America would become involved in a worldwide "witch-hunt." From then on, they claimed, America's allies would be determined by how loudly a nation claimed to be fighting communism. Taylor believed that Franco, Perón, Chiang Kai-shek, and other reactionaries were rejoicing over the new turn of events in America. It was the Idaho liberal's conviction that if the United States was so willing to assist "reactionary regimes" (Greece and Turkey) in the name of anti-communism, the American-Soviet split would widen.[20]

The two future Progressive leaders begged Americans to develop a degree of empathy. How would Americans feel if Russia poured millions of dollars into Mexico and Cuba? This was exactly what the United States was doing in Greece and Turkey. What other course could the Russians take except to bolster their defenses in the Balkans and in southern Russia? To Wallace and Taylor the future looked very dismal, for they believed the two superpowers were pushing each other toward atomic destruction. In spite of the grim warnings, the Senate approved the Truman

[19] *New York Times*, April 5, 1947, p. 6.
[20] *Cong. Rec.*, 80th Cong., 1st sess., 1947, 93, pt. 3:3404–3407.

Doctrine by a 67–23 margin on April 22.[21] Henry Wallace's words on the precedent set by the Truman Doctrine were direct and prophetic: "President Truman cannot prevent change in the world any more than he can prevent the tide from coming in or the sun from rising. But once America stands for opposition to change we are lost. America will become the most hated nation in the world."[22]

The senatorial debate over the Truman Doctrine had scarcely begun to subside when Secretary of State George C. Marshall dropped another rhetorical bomb. Speaking at the Harvard commencement on June 5, Marshall called for Europe to cooperate with the United States in a titanic economic rehabilitation effort for devastated and war-torn nations.[23] Marshall was not a gifted orator, but in a fifteen-minute address he outlined concisely what came to be called the Marshall Plan. Committing the United States to full European recovery, the secretary explained: "Our policy is directed not against any country or doctrine but against hunger, poverty, desperation, and chaos. Any assistance this country may render in the future should provide a cure rather than a mere palliative. Any government that is willing to assist in the task of recovery will find full cooperation."[24]

Glen Taylor disapproved of the proposed Marshall Plan for reasons similar to those he voiced when voting against the Truman Doctrine. Admitting that Europe needed help in order to rebuild, Taylor believed the United Nations, rather than individual nations, should administer the relief.[25] To reporters, the Idaho Democrat stated: "I am all for preventing the people of the world from starving. But our present program is not predicated

21 Ibid., p. 3497.
22 *New York Times*, March 14, 1947, p. 7.
23 *Cong. Rec.*, 80th Cong., 1st sess., 1947, 93, pt. 12:A3248. See also the *New York Times*, June 6, 1947, p. 1.
24 *New York Times*, June 6, 1947, p. 1.
25 Ibid., June 23, 1947, p. 5.

on this but on gaining selfish political ends. The Hindus are starving, but there is no thought of aiding them, because there is no 'communist threat' to worry us."[26] Taylor also expressed a fear that the Soviet Union would react adversely to the Marshall Plan by making Eastern Europe more dependent on the Russians for economic survival.[27] Taylor's apprehensions proved justified when the Soviet Union refused to participate in the Marshall Plan because, according to Russian spokesmen, the European nations would become mere economic satellites of the United States.[28]

By the fall of 1947, after the Russians had announced their counter Molotov Plan, Wallace was likewise critical of the Marshall Plan. In late December he told a Milwaukee audience that the national general welfare was being sacrificed to the interests of the financial and industrial tycoons who controlled both parties. He referred to the European Recovery Program, the official title of the Marshall Plan, as "a plan to interfere in the social, economic, and political affairs of countries receiving aid." The plan also allied the American people with "kings, fascists, and reactionaries."[29] Specifically, Wallace believed that the United Nations should handle rehabilitation, that loans should be unconditional, and that money received should not be used for military purposes.

The Marshall proposal would not reach the Senate floor until the spring of 1948, but Taylor and Wallace kept up their barrage of verbal opposition. Deeply disturbed by the Truman

[26] *Daily Worker* (New York), November 21, 1947, p. 2.
[27] *Lewiston Morning Tribune* (Lewiston, Idaho), October 5, 1947, p. 1.
[28] *New York Times*, July 3, 1947, p. 4, notes the objection of Foreign Minister Vyacheslav Molotov. The same objections were voiced by Andrei Vishinsky, chairman of the Soviet Delegation to the United Nations, ibid., September 19, 1947, pp. 18–19.
[29] *New York Times*, December 31, 1947, p. 1.

policies, Taylor decided to go west and see how his constituents felt about the new developments. After a short stay, Taylor was convinced that the people wanted peace above all else. He decided to dramatize the issues by resorting to a theatrical stunt— a horseback ride across the nation. Although an equestrian continental traversal seemed an unusual way to determine public opinion, Taylor frankly told reporters: "I've spent most of my life on stage and I realize that in order to attract attention to a voice which opposes our foreign policy, I must dramatize the issue."[30] Public response to Taylor's ride from California to Texas reinforced his belief that Truman's policies were courting disaster. He returned to Washington in November, 1947, and made a decision that led him briefly to political prominence and eventually to obscurity.

On December 29, 1947, Henry A. Wallace officially and dramatically announced that he would form a new party and seek the American presidency, and within two months he had persuaded the disenchanted Taylor to accept the vice-presidential nomination. There is no doubt that Truman's foreign policy, epitomized by the Marshall Plan, was a major factor in the Wallace decision. In the solemn tones of an evangelist, Wallace declared to a national radio audience: "We have assembled a Gideon's Army, small in number, powerful in conviction, ready for action. We have said with Gideon, 'Let those who are fearful and trembling depart.' For every fearful one who leaves, there will be a thousand to take his place. A just cause is worth a hundred armies. We face the future unfettered, unfettered by any principle but the general welfare. By God's grace, the people's peace will usher in the century of the common man."[31]

Taylor echoed: "We dare not falter, because a few steps down

---

[30] *Lewiston Morning Tribune*, October 21, 1947, p. 1. See "Glen Taylor's Ride," *Newsweek*, October 24, 1947, pp. 26–27.

[31] *New York Times*, December 30, 1947, p. 1.

the road we are presently traveling lurks oblivion."[32] With these
clarion calls, backed by liberal labor leaders, civil rights groups,
and the Communist party of the United States, the new Progressive party charted a course designed to bring peace and prosperity.

Following the solidification of their national ticket, Wallace
and Taylor prepared separate courses of action. Wallace attempted to outline positive programs designed to achieve international
peace and domestic equality. Taylor was the new party's devil's
advocate. One of his duties, from the Progressive standpoint,
was to engage in a continuous attack on the Truman foreign
policies, especially the Marshall Plan.

Less than two weeks after Taylor openly announced his support of Wallace, he obtained the Senate floor and began a lengthy
discussion of the Marshall Plan. The new Progressive told his
colleagues that the United States was not trying to give economic
assistance to Europe, but instead was attempting to dominate all
of Western Europe economically. According to Taylor, the Truman Doctrine and the Marshall Plan, if enacted, would make the
United Nations powerless and useless.[33] Utilizing an opportunity
to let loose a thrust at what he considered the true enemies of
peace in America—the anti-Communist extremists, Taylor said:
"The glory of spending money to fight communism commands
such attention in the press of America that even to bask in the
reflection of the spot light throws an aura upon all those who
can even get close to the center of the stage."[34] Taylor blamed
the "reactionary press, the generals and admirals, big figures in
the finance and business world and, of course, those politicians
who like to go with the tide" for creating a "tidal wave of sup-

[32] *Spokesman-Review* (Spokane, Washington), February 24, 1948,
p. 2.
[33] *Cong. Rec.*, 80th Cong., 2nd sess., 1948, 94, pt. 2:2387.
[34] Ibid.

port to [give] away billions and billions to try to bribe people not to be Communists."[35]

Taylor continued his speech against the Marshall Plan with the declaration that the United States had not earnestly tried to achieve peace with the Russians and, before the administration formed economic and military alliances, it should at least attempt direct negotiations with the Soviets. Admitting that his position was based on the assumption "that the Russians are not absolutely hopeless, and that it is possible to get along with them," Taylor acknowledged that by taking this stance he was laying himself "open to the charge of being a Communist—a Communist sympathizer, at least."[36] Before taking his seat, the Idaho senator was assured that when the Senate reconvened the next day, he would again have the floor.

The next morning, Taylor introduced a substitute bill for the Marshall Plan. This piece of legislation was drafted by Wallace and his advisors and proposed a positive alternative to unilateral aid to be given to certain "pet" nations. Taylor began his remarks with the customary Progressive affirmation of loyalty to the United States. Declaring America by far the best nation on earth, he said: "If I did not love my country, if I were willing to see it destroyed, I would skip the whole thing."[37] But, in Taylor's view, the true patriot must remain an objective critic of himself and his country. Speaking to only eleven colleagues, but to a packed gallery, he solemnly continued: "If I were easily terrified, I would turn my back on [the] struggle . . . and make my peace. I cannot do that. For the sake of my wife and children, I almost wish I could. . . . We cannot save ourselves by hiding in the mob and joining in the clamor because in another war the

35 Ibid.
36 Ibid.
37 Ibid., p. 2453.

mob will be destroyed—all of us."[38] Then Taylor placed before the Senate the Progressives' "Peace and Reconstruction Act of 1948," a bill, he said, designed to repudiate the militaristic and imperialistic implications of the Truman Doctrine and the Marshall Plan by channeling all funds through the United Nations. Economic rehabilitation, the aim of the Marshall Plan, was to be financed by contributions from the member nations of the United Nations, with top priority for aid going to those nations which had suffered the most during the war, including both Germany and Russia. Calling the Progressive proposal a bill for peace and reconstruction, Taylor claimed that the Marshall Plan was a bill that prepared for war and put Europe on a permanent dole. He concluded: "If the American people could choose freely, they would choose peace, not war; for genuine reconstruction, not permanent poverty."[39]

The Progressives' substitute bill, which was not taken seriously, was defeated seventy-four to three the same day. Shortly thereafter the Marshall Plan won approval by a voice vote.[40]

Progressive dissent from Truman's policies led to one of the most interesting and controversial occurrences of the cold war. On March 17, 1948, near the end of his special message to Congress, Harry Truman asked for passage of the European Recovery Program, universal military training, and a new selective service act. Near the end of his speech, the President stated: "The door has never been closed, nor will it ever be closed, to the Soviet

[38] Ibid., p. 2454.
[39] Ibid., p. 2458. The Progressive criticism was published in a pamphlet entitled *The Wallace Plan or the Marshall Plan.* Progressive party file, New York Public Library.
[40] *Cong. Rec.,* 80th Cong., 2nd sess., 1948, 94, pt. 2:2749. Joseph M. Jones, *The Fifteen Weeks* (New York: Viking Press, 1955), discusses the effect of the Czechoslovakian coup on the Marshall Plan debates.

Union or any other nation that will genuinely cooperate in preserving the peace."[41]

After reading the Truman speech, American Ambassador to the Soviet Union General Walter Bedell Smith told Soviet Foreign Minister V. M. Molotov: "As far as the United States is concerned, the door is always open for full discussion and the composing of our differences."[42] According to Secretary of State Marshall, Smith's statement reflected the Truman policymakers' concern over the possible effect of Henry Wallace's campaign and was intended as an indication to the Soviet leaders that Wallace's foreign-policy ideas had no chance of adoption by the Truman administration; the United States had absolutely no intention of inviting the Soviets to a conference.[43]

Five days after receipt of the Smith proposal, Molotov replied: "The Soviet government views favorably the desire of the government of the United States to improve . . . relations . . . and agrees to the proposal to proceed with this end in view, to a discussion and settlement of the differences existing between us." Molotov released both statements to the press, an act which American diplomats viewed as a breach of diplomacy—but the world breathed a sigh of relief.[44]

Without openly repudiating the ambassador, Truman simply stated: "The policies of the United States government have been

[41] Barton Bernstein and Allen J. Matusow, eds., *The Truman Administration: A Documentary History* (New York: Harper and Row, 1968), p. 221.
[42] *New York Times*, May 11, 1948, pp. 1–2. See MacDougall, *Gideon's Army*, pp. 351–361, and Schmidt, *Henry A. Wallace*, pp. 75–78, for brief accounts of the Smith-Molotov and the Wallace-Stalin exchanges.
[43] *New York Times*, May 12, 1948, pp. 1–8, and May 13, 1948, p. 1.
[44] Ibid. On May 13 both the *Chicago Daily News* and the *New York Post* said in editorials that the Truman administration would be foolish not to follow up on the Smith-Molotov feelers.

made amply clear in recent months and weeks. . . . They will
continue to be vigorously and firmly prosecuted." Marshall said
that neither he nor Smith was a diplomat, but he confirmed the
administration's apprehension over the impact of the Wallace
initiative. Administration sources dismissed the Soviet reply as
"economically motivated"—a desire to receive American aid.[45]

The Progressive party decided to pursue the negotiations and,
in an unprecedented move, Wallace sent an open letter to Joseph
Stalin. Calling for a return to "the war-time cooperation between
the two great powers," Wallace presented his thoughts on the
steps "necessary to achieve the Century of Peace."[46] Wallace proposed a series of "definite, decisive" measures to end the cold
war. The list included a general reduction of armaments, the
outlawing of all methods of mass destruction, a halt in the export
of weapons, and the resumption of unrestricted trade between
the two nations. Wallace intended to create a better understanding among Americans, Russians, and other peoples of the world.
He therefore proposed the free movement of American and
Soviet citizens between the two nations, as well as freedom of
movement within the host country. Recognizing the Russian fear
caused by America's atomic monopoly, Wallace called for the
free exchange of scientific information and material plus United
Nations control of atomic energy. In the letter to Stalin, Wallace
specifically asked for an early peace treaty with both Germany
and Japan, withdrawal of all troops from Korea, a "hands-off"
policy toward China, and statements by both major powers that
neither had designs on the territorial integrity of any other nation.[47]

Convinced that the Soviets genuinely wanted peace, Wallace
concluded the letter as follows: "There is no misunderstanding

45 *New York Times*, May 12, 1948, pp. 1, 8.
46 Ibid., pp. 1, 14.
47 Ibid.

or difficulty between the U.S.A. and the U.S.S.R. which can be settled by force or fear and there is no difference which cannot be settled by peaceful, hopeful negotiation. There is no American principle or public interest, and there is no Russian principle or public interest which would have to be sacrificed to end the cold war and open up the Century of Peace which the Century of the Common Man demands."[48]

The intrusion of a private citizen into a tense cold-war diplomatic impasse did nothing to ease the situation. It might even be argued that the administration failed to follow up on the Smith-Molotov feelers because of Wallace's open letter. Newspapers did report that Truman would send Chief Justice Fred Vinson to Moscow, but the Vinson mission did not materialize.

The full impact of Wallace's letter to Stalin did not become apparent for about one week—until Stalin responded directly to Wallace over Moscow radio. The Soviet dictator described the Wallace proposals as serious steps toward a "concrete program for peaceful settlement of the differences between the U.S.S.R. and the United States."[49] Stalin admitted that despite the differences in the economic systems and ideologies, the coexistence of these systems was "not only possible but also doubtlessly necessary in the interest of a general peace."[50]

The Truman administration did not consider the Wallace initiative and the Stalin response diplomatically significant. Marshall commented that the Stalin position, while encouraging, was really meaningless, because all issues previously had been discussed in the United Nations, and he perceived no basis for bilateral negotiations.

When he heard of the administration attitude, Wallace was beside himself. Speaking in Seattle, he forcefully denounced

[48] Ibid.
[49] Ibid., May 18, 1948, pp. 1, 4.
[50] Ibid.

American policy: "If we recognize the fundamental fact that American foreign policy today is based on serving private corporations and international big business, rather than serving great masses of people—when we recognize this fact we can understand their unwillingness to reach agreement with Russia."[51] As Wallace watched his lone-wolf peace course shunted into obscurity, he quietly observed, "If my letter has served and can still serve to further international understanding of the issues and the practicability of peace, I consider that this past two years' work has been truly fruitful."[52]

Once again the potential appeal of the coexistence theme was undercut as mellow Russian words gave way to harsh Soviet actions. Many Americans who had thought it possible for the United States and the Soviet Union to live as peaceful friends in a new world were convinced by the Czechoslovakian coup in 1948 that the Soviets had resumed their long-range plans for world conquests. That conviction was reinforced by a second crisis, this time in Berlin, deep in the Russian sector of East Germany. Initially, the problem stemmed from an attempt to reform German currency, but it developed into a Communist blockade of Berlin. Truman's response was an immediate order to supply the city by a gigantic airlift.

Viewed in this light, the Progressive party's peace proposals and talk of solving Russo-American difficulties rang a bit hollow. Futility and appeasement were words often used to describe the Progressive party's course. Because of these international developments, many potential supporters concluded it wiser to remain loyal to their old parties. Thus, Soviet behavior in both Czechoslovakia and Berlin undermined Henry Wallace's positive attempt to cut through the cold-war ice.

An integral part of Harry Truman's foreign policy was his

[51] Ibid., May 22, 1948, p. 7.
[52] Schmidt, *Henry A. Wallace*, p. 77.

conviction that force should be met with force. Thus, in March of 1948, he had requested bipartisan support for his proposal to resume selective service and inaugurate universal military training. The president's recommendations were predicated on what he believed was an unmistakable policy on the part of the Soviet Union to create international chaos. In his address before a joint session of Congress, Truman stated: "The adoption of universal training by the United States at this time would be unmistakable evidence to all the world of our determination to back the will to peace with the strength for peace."[53] Contending that it was impossible to meet our international responsibilities without maintaining a large armed force, the president proclaimed the necessity of keeping occupation armies in Europe and Asia until peace was secured.

Truman's conscription and universal military training bills were not greeted by riots, draft-card burnings, or the mass movement of potential draftees to foreign soil, yet, like all draft legislation, they were not completely popular. There were no organized attempts to thwart the workings of selective service boards. Student protesters, Dr. Benjamin Spock, university chaplains, and dissident priests were saving their oratorical batteries and organizational abilities for another generation; however, there was opposition, and it was led by Henry Wallace and Glen Taylor.

It would be three months before peacetime conscription actually came before the Senate for consideration, but the day after Truman's message, Taylor warned his colleagues that he would fight any such proposal: "If the President meant that we must all unite for military training, if he meant that all political factions must unite to reimpose the draft upon the American people—if that is what the President meant, . . . I can guarantee that there

[53] Bernstein and Matusow, *A Documentary History*, pp. 270–271.

will be political opposition, that there will not be unanimity, and although we may not be permitted to carry on for a very long period of time, we shall certainly fight the drive toward war, this surrender to Wall Street and the military, to our last breath of freedom."[54] The Idaho senator concluded with a pointed denunciation of the entire diplomatic course being followed by the administration and asserted that it reminded him of Germany during the 1930's.

Wallace immediately attacked the UMT bill because of its economics. Claiming that domestic needs should be given top priority, the Progressive candidate speculated that the money spent on universal military training could (1) build a school, library, and hospital in every county of the nation; or (2) provide nurses, full-time health services, and a new schoolhouse in every county; or (3) provide facilities and guidance for recreation, and build and maintain tuition-free junior colleges in every county; or (4) provide educational facilities for at least three million young people a year who were not then receiving education; or (5) build a trade and technical school in every congressional district in the nation.[55] Wallace's logic was lost on a nation determined above all else to halt the apparent spread of communism.

Glen Taylor, Progressive leader of the attack in the Senate against the Marshall Plan, spoke against universal military training and conscription when those issues reached the Senate floor in June, 1948. Amply supplied with material from Progressive researchers, Taylor based his arguments against the draft and universal military training on five major premises. First, that a peacetime draft was a clear break with American tradition. Second, Taylor feared that conscription and universal military training would assist in the creation of a mammoth military complex,

[54] *Cong. Rec.*, 80th Cong., 2nd sess., 1948, 94, pt. 3:2993.
[55] The *Oregonian* (Portland), May 25, 1948, p. 1.

keeping the economy geared to military rather than needed consumer production. His third reason was based on the following question: "With atomic bombs available to threaten annihilation, why have a large army?" Fourth, the Idaho senator maintained that the commander in chief should use his executive power to integrate the existing armed forces and eliminate racial discrimination in the military service, before any more black citizens were drafted into a third-class status; and finally, he contended, the resumption of military training was an admission to the world that America was arming for war and that her foreign policy had failed. When it became evident that peacetime conscription would be approved, Taylor joined William Langer of North Dakota in a Senate filibuster against a resumption of selective service, again in vain.

An analysis of Senator Taylor's rhetoric reveals his basic humanitarian sense. He abhorred the idea of a large standing army and the possibility of an economy based on armament production. He charged that the State Department was controlled by representatives of the military and Wall Street, and asked, "Do they want to get us into war, or do they want to keep us just short of war so that there will be billions spent on armaments?"[56] Using simple terms, he warned the nation against a military-industrial complex: "Once it is saddled on us it will be impossible to get rid of it, because when a large segment of our industry is making guns, tanks, and planes, jobs will depend on making guns, tanks, and planes, and profits will depend on making guns, tanks, and planes." Grimly insisting on the permanence of the draft and an armament economy, once accepted, he said, "I fail to find in history any instance where a country built up a great arms establishment and did away with it without using it. In other words, we are getting into quicksand; when we get in

[56] *Daily Worker*, October 10, 1947, p. 5.

so far, it will be impossible to get out."[57] Taylor concluded his
denunciation of the "vested interests" with the cynical observa-
tion that the economy as presently constituted could without
doubt survive another war, but he feared what would happen "if
peace broke out."[58]

The threat of nuclear war seems to have loomed larger on the
Taylor horizon than the domestic impact of the Truman pre-
paredness program. It seems to have been the primary reason
that he and Wallace divorced themselves from the Democrats.
Both constantly bemoaned the fact that the United States continued to stockpile atomic weapons. During the draft filibuster,
Taylor caustically declared: "Inasmuch as we have . . . enough
bombs to kill everyone in the world, including ourselves, I fail
to see the percentage in starting a war. We are all going to die if
a war were to come."[59] Of the draft and universal military training, he had bluntly said, "there is no need for this idiotic draft
. . . because we have enough atomic bombs to kill everybody in
the world, so I do not see that it makes any difference whether
we draft them first or kill them first."[60] Fearing the threat of
atomic annihilation, the 1948 Progressives believed it best to try
for peace, even if it meant joining Don Quixote in front of the
windmills.

Supporting his argument that resumption of military training
was tacit admission that United States foreign policy was not
working, Taylor contended that the Truman policy, denigrating
the United Nations as only a "paper tiger" and launching the
United States on an arms race, was losing America friends around
the world, especially among the emerging nations of Africa and
Asia. To Taylor, it was very simple: in supporting reactionary

[57] *Cong. Rec.*, 80th Cong., 2nd sess., 1948, 94, pt. 6:7586.
[58] Ibid., pt. 7:8780.
[59] Ibid., p. 8781.
[60] Ibid., p. 8802.

"cardboard governments" throughout the world, American diplomacy was "helping bad people everywhere." He used the example of China, where, he said, "we are helping Chiang Kaishek, whose government is so corrupt that it takes a part of the guns we send them to fight the Communists and sells them to the Communists. That keeps the Communists in business, which scares us so badly that we send China more guns, which are sold to the Communists, and we are scared some more, so we send China more guns."[61]

The Progressives' attempt to curb militarization ended in failure, as had their earlier undertaking against the Marshall Plan and the Truman Doctrine. Although the universal military training proposal was defeated, congressional approval for resuming selective service was easily obtained, and, as the summer of 1948 turned into autumn, the Progressive crusade of Henry Wallace lost its early zeal. Most of the Progressive critics of Truman's cold-war policies suffered devastating defeat at the polls.[62] Undoubtedly the "soft on communism" charge hurled at the Wallace party injured it severely. In an era when the nation was ripe for a Joseph McCarthy and already convinced that communism was the ultimate evil, in a time when the United States and the Soviet Union appeared to perch on the brink of atomic war, the support of the Progressives by the American Communists certainly dashed any hopes for a successful effort.[63] The Communists' coup in Czechoslovakia, the Berlin blockade, and the beginning of the Communist Chinese victory, the Alger Hiss–Whittaker Chambers affair, the arrest of the American Communist leaders—all during 1948—made the Wallace–Taylor speeches sound like naive appeasement. Anything remotely connected with

[61] Ibid., pt. 6:7588.
[62] Schmidt, *Henry A. Wallace*, pp. 327–335.
[63] Ibid., p. 248.

communism in 1948 spelled doom, and the Progressives were categorized by the press and both major parties as "reds."

Henry Wallace launched his party with the intent of preserving peace. He believed that his party should be remembered as an attempt to prevent World War III and to create a better America, not as a conspiracy by the Communists to assume power. The dissent of the Progressives against the prevailing Truman foreign policy has traditionally been viewed as an effort designed to appease the Russians, but recent historical scholarship places the Progressive position in a different light. In fact, these new studies basically agree with the Progressives' criticisms of Truman's actions.

Instead of placing the entire blame for the cold war on the shoulders of the Russians, monographs by revisionist historians in recent years demonstrate that the responsibility must be shared.[64] Generally, these historians view the cold war as a series of over-reactions on the part of the Soviets, the Americans, the British, and the French. With the benefit of historical hindsight, they argue that the frigid post-war conditions were the result of attempts by both power blocs to preempt political and economic dominance over neighboring or friendly governments. The emergence of a power struggle between the Soviet Union and the United States coincided with the surge of nationalism sweeping through the colonial empires of the Netherlands, Great Britain, and France. The ideological and military tension almost demand-

---

[64] Historians advocating this point of view include Walter LaFeber, William A. Williams, Ronald Steel, David Horowitz, Gar Alperovitz, Barton Bernstein, and Thomas Paterson. Alperovitz's *Atomic Diplomacy: Hiroshima and Potsdam* (New York: Random House, 1965) is a very controversial book on the purpose of the atomic bomb. Paterson has edited *Cold War Critics* (Chicago: Quadrangle, 1971) and *The Origins of the Cold War* (Boston: D. C. Heath, 1970) and has just completed a work on the economic causes of the cold war.

ed that the new nations make a choice. In the bipolarized world, neutrals were suspect. All of these factors contributed to the very complex post-war world of 1948.

The revisionist historians are most critical of Truman because of the development of a warfare state. Perhaps the most relevant cause espoused by Wallace and the new party was opposition to the growing military-industrial alliance. Long before the warning by retiring President Dwight D. Eisenhower concerning the military-industrial complex, the Progressives realized that America was undergoing a basic change that involved a reversal of priorities—a change of the American dream. After accepting the new party's nomination, Henry Wallace emphatically declared: "The American dream is no utopian vision. We do not plan rocket ships for weekend trips to Mars. The dream is the hard and simple truth of what can be done. In one fleet of heavy bombers lies wealth and skill . . . that could have taken a million veterans out of trailer camps and chicken coops. We can build new schools to rescue our children from the firetraps where they now crowd. . . . We can end the murderous tyranny of sickness and disease. The dream is nothing but the facts. The facts are that we spend $20 billion a year for cold war." [65]

This dramatic reorientation of the American dream was also illustrated by James Forrestal, Truman's secretary of defense in 1948, when he spoke to the first graduating class of the Armed Forces Information School. Forrestal told the graduates that their task would be difficult because "our democracy and our country are founded upon an underlying suspicion of armies and of the force that they reflect and represent. . . . Part of your task is to make people realize that the Army, Navy, and Air Force are not external creations but come from and are part of the people. It

[65] *Cong. Rec.*, 80th Cong., 2nd sess., 1948, 94, pt. 12:A5907.

is your responsibility to make citizens aware of their responsibility to the service."[66] For the first time in our history, citizens had to be aware of their responsibility to the military! Universal military training, which the Progressives opposed so bitterly, was an attempt to complete the reversal of the roles of master and servant.

It can still be debated, as the Progressives contended in 1948, that the military, aided by big business, has acquired unprecedented influence in foreign and domestic affairs. Its degree of control of the national economy since World War II is indicated by the proportion of the federal budget it receives. But a more serious charge has been made. It is that the military-industrial alliance encouraged the cold war in order to maintain a permanent war economy and avoid domestic recessions. Through a powerful propaganda web the military-industrial complex created national emergencies and international fear, thus promoting the arms race and justifying unnecessary offense spending.[67] Fear is the basest of human emotions, and in 1957 retired General Douglas MacArthur offered a caustic commentary on the previous decade. His remarks are still pertinent: "Our government has kept us in a perpetual state of fear—kept us in a continued stampede of patriotic fervor—with the cry of a grave national emergency. . . . Yet, in retrospect, these disasters seem never to have happened, seem never to have been quite real."[68] The inability to differentiate between the real and the contrived still plagues this nation, as Cambodia, Laos, and the alleged submarine base in Cuba attest.

Proponents of and apologists for the development of a warfare state argue that it was absolutely necessary to contain Communist

[66] Fred Cook, *The Warfare State* (New York: Macmillan Co., 1962), p. 108.
[67] Ibid., pp. 95–99, 110–125.
[68] Ibid., p. 175.

expansion. Wallace and Taylor not only disagreed, but also vehe-
mently opposed the instrumentalities of containment: the Truman Doctrine, the Marshall Plan, and universal military training.
Wallace believed that containment was a mere smokescreen behind which American business could dominate economically the
rehabilitation of war-torn Europe and Asia. Just as the ghost of
Peter the Great was responsible for Soviet behavior in Eastern
Europe, so the ghost of John Hay and the Open Door policy
were accountable for American actions. As Truman pointed out
prior to enunciating the doctrine that bears his name, "the pattern of international trade which is most conducive to freedom
of enterprise is one in which major decisions are made not by
governments but by private buyers and sellers." There was little
doubt that America had emerged from the war as the leader of
the economic world, and the Truman administration believed it
must make the choice whether or not to sustain and expand
private enterprise. Simultaneously, it was necessary to avoid a
domestic depression and the political consequences thereof.
Again, the Progressives seem close to the true intent of the Truman policy.

If the Truman Doctrine and the Marshall Plan helped push
Harry Truman up the presidential rating ladder, long-term analysis of the same policies might contribute to the Wallace–Taylor
contemporary assessment. Most historians still view Truman's
policy as the savior of the Western nations. Greece, free from
communism, was a worthy goal, but a reactionary government
still exists there, and it is obvious that our concern stretched clear
into the oil-rich Middle East. In order to keep the oil trade in
the proper hands, the United States was found cooperating with
the reactionary Arab leaders, the American oil interests, and the
British imperialists. The Marshall Plan was billed as a great ex-
pression of America's inherent humanitarianism and it did represent a generous urge to assist the battle-weary masses of Western

Europe. It is noteworthy that China, India, and Latin America were excluded from Marshall Plan assistance, even though from both a humanitarian and a policy point of view their needs were great.[69] Disposing of America's "great surplus" offered a new economic frontier to American capitalists, as well as an opportunity to support free enterprise at home. Marshall believed that unless his plan was adopted, "the cumulative loss of foreign markets and sources of supply would unquestionably have a depressing influence on our domestic economy and would drive us to increased measures of governmental control."[70] The very difficult question remains: Were the Marshall Plan and the Truman Doctrine inspired by a desire to contain communism or were they designed to ensure American economic stability?[71]

Generally it can be concluded concerning the origins and causes of the cold war that neither power bloc was blameless. This is exactly the position taken by the Progressives in 1948. The sad indictment of America's policies, right or wrong, is that most such early critics as Henry Wallace and Glen Taylor were emphatically discredited as being either Communist-sympathizers or idealistic dreamers. Taking into consideration what most Americans, including Harry Truman, believed to be true in 1948 (an international Communist conspiracy was attempting to take over the world), it is no small wonder that the Progressives were trounced by the masses they attempted to reach. On the other hand, discerning the obvious Russian fear (an aggressive United States was attempting to control the world economically, politically, and militarily), Soviet behavior in Eastern Europe is understandable.

Presidents will always be rated, and the criteria used will fluc-

[69] Williams, *Tragedy of American Diplomacy*, pp. 270–271.
[70] Ibid., p. 271.
[71] Ibid. See also LaFeber, *America, Russia, and the Cold War*, pp. 47–51.

tuate with the specific historian and with the times. Harry Truman's fortunes may fall and then rise again at a future date. He led the nation during tumultuous years, and when a common man presides in times of crisis, it can breed greatness. Perhaps legitimate criteria for judging Truman's presidency and his foreign policy were outlined by Henry A. Wallace in the early morning hours after Truman's upset victory in 1948. Writing with a blunt pencil on the back of a mimeographed copy of his congratulatory telegram, the defeated Progressive party candidate discussed the challenge facing Truman:

You now have a unique opportunity to unite the world on the basis of putting millions to work providing peacetime goods who are now forging the instruments of destruction. Peace with honor is possible. Peace with complete security and without appeasement is possible. . . . Will you now take the next step and prove to the people of the world that the U.S. is finally ready to build for world peace? . . . I am convinced that you can include in the Peace Treaty with Russia provision for permitting and encouraging full peacetime use of atomic energy for power while at the same time the human race is preserved from a return to barbarism by effective supervision to eliminate all possibility for the construction and stockpiling of atomic weapons. . . . The destiny and salvation of the U.S. is to serve the world—not dominate it. By moving . . . in this direction you can become America's greatest President. You will become great by the enemies you make as you serve the people of this nation and the whole world at peace.[72]

According to Wallace's criteria, Truman failed to measure up, and, in retrospect, the Truman foreign policy may have left a legacy of superweapons, imperialism, and domestic apprehensions. Truman dedicated himself to new housing, civil rights, reclamation, national health insurance, and aid to education, yet these domestic problems still cry for solution. Was the contain-

[72] MacDougall, *Gideon's Army*, III, 884.

ment philosophy father to Vietnam and Cambodia and Laos? Will the heritage of the Truman administration be one of opportunities lost and energies wasted? Let time and the historians who rate presidents decide. Henry Wallace and Glen Taylor drew their own conclusions.

JOHN COLLIER
AND THE AMERICAN INDIAN, 1920-1945

BY KENNETH R. PHILP

ON APRIL 21, 1933, President Franklin Roosevelt confirmed the appointment of John Collier as Commissioner of Indian Affairs. One of the most colorful of the New Dealers, Collier was a small stoop-shouldered man who wore glasses and kept his blond hair long and unbrushed. At the Indian Bureau office he smoked a corncob pipe which he often placed in an empty water glass on his desk. Instead of wearing a jacket, Collier came to work in "a baggy old long-sleeved green sweater." A contemporary thought that he looked like a country storekeeper closing out the week's accounts. Gossips in Washington also rumored that this unconventional man sometimes carried a pet frog in his pocket.[1]

Secretary of the Interior Harold Ickes had appointed Collier as the new Indian commissioner because he believed him to be "the best equipped man who ever held this office."[2] Collier's previous

[1] "Indian Fighter," *Time*, February 19, 1945, pp. 18–19; and "People in the Limelight," *New Republic*, March 5, 1945, p. 319.
[2] *New York Times*, April 16, 1933, p. 10.

career substantiated Ickes's evaluation. Born in Atlanta in 1884 to a union of southern and New England families, Collier had attended Columbia University and the Collège de France at Paris. While at Columbia in 1902, he came under the influence of Miss Lucy Crozier, a free-lance New York teacher, who helped him formulate a social philosophy which would eventually direct his interest toward the American Indian.[3]

Miss Crozier exposed Collier to many of the ideas associated with the neoromantic intellectual revolution at the turn of the century. This reorientation of European social thought dealt with the problem of irrational motivation in human conduct.[4] Like many of his contemporaries, Collier rejected the biological and mechanistic determinism found in the tenets of Social Darwinism. He revolted against free-market and laissez-faire doctrines portraying the human world as an aggregation of persons controlled by universal economic laws. Collier also cast aside all values which justified wealth as an end in itself and instead focused upon subjective and spiritual motivations in history.[5]

According to Collier, there were four epochs in history. They included prehistory, the classical-Christian period, the advent of modern science, and the industrial age. He believed that through all of prehistory the individual had depended on the small group for existence. The common man felt a social purpose because he realized that he was society. Then came the classical period, which witnessed the growth of large centralized states and cities. The

[3] John Collier, *From Every Zenith* (Denver: Sage Books, 1963), pp. 1–40.

[4] Consult H. Stuart Hughes, *Consciousness and Society: The Reorientation of European Social Thought, 1890–1930* (New York: Alfred A. Knopf, 1958), and Henry F. May, *The End of American Innocence* (New York: Alfred A. Knopf, 1959).

[5] John Collier, "Organized Laity and the Social Expert: The Meaning of Public Community Centers," *National Conference on Social Work* (1917), pp. 465–469.

common man no longer felt that the destinies of the world rested on his shoulders, but the growth of Christianity once again enabled him to identify with the hope of mankind. This association with social purpose, however, started to disintegrate with the beginning of modern science.[6]

The dilemma of modern man in the fourth epoch of history, the industrial age, especially concerned Collier. He worried about the impact of industrialization and urbanization on the quality of human life. He realized that organic society, with its sense of community, was being replaced by one which isolated the individual. Collier felt that the supremacy of machine over man led only to the uprooting of populations, the disintegration of neighborhoods, and the starvation of the soul.[7]

Because of his interest in creating a sense of community, Collier became a social worker in New York City in 1907. He worked as civic secretary of the People's Institute, which attempted to give the immigrant masses a sense of brotherhood in local neighborhood communities. Founded in 1897 by Charles Sprague Smith, former head of Columbia University's department of comparative literature, the Institute tried "to give knowledge, leadership, and public voice to the wage earning masses." Collier's activities included editing the Institute's newspaper, the *Civic Journal*, which promoted the causes of labor, public ownership of transportation, and the reform program of Tammany Hall opponent Mayor William Jay Gaynor. Collier also persuaded the New York City Board of Education to keep its schools open after hours for use as community centers, and he established a training school for community workers.[8]

---

[6] Ibid.

[7] John Collier, *Indians of the Americas*, abridged ed. (New York: New American Library, 1947), pp. 12–16.

[8] John Collier, "People's Institute," *Independent*, May 30, 1912, pp. 1144–1148; and Collier, *From Every Zenith*, pp. 68–94.

While at the People's Institute, Collier unknowingly formulated ideas which later proved crucial in dealing with the American Indian. He believed that dignity and power for the average person, the future of leisure and of realized life, could be ensured only by revitalizing and enriching the primary social group until it was adequate to human nature, and that, to this end, the preservation and nurture of ethnic values was essential.[9] Collier thought that only organized groups of people, joined in tasks of cooperative self-expression and social service, could discover a new state of social consciousness and thus save man from the negative consequences of the industrial age. Within a few years he began to realize that the American Indian could help accomplish this goal.

Seeing his social work in New York City negated by the Americanization drive of World War I, Collier moved to California in 1919 to undertake the leadership of that state's adult-education program. One year later, under surveillance by Department of Justice agents during the red scare because of his lectures concerning the development of community and the Russian Revolution, he resigned his California position and decided to visit the wilderness of Mexico.[10] But his trip was to be permanently interrupted when Mabel Dodge, a bohemian whose prewar salon in Greenwich Village he had attended, invited him to visit the Indian pueblo at Taos, New Mexico.[11]

Intermittently through the next two years, Collier occupied a house in the art colony at Spanish American Taos, two miles from the Indian pueblo. Evening conversations with artists and writers around the fireplace at the Dodge home soon enlisted

[9] Laura Thompson, "John Collier: Biographical Sketch," John Collier Papers, Western Americana Collection, Yale University Library [n.d.] (hereafter referred to as the Collier Papers), pp. 1–3.
[10] Collier, *From Every Zenith*, pp. 1–3.
[11] Ibid.

Collier in the movement to revive and preserve Indian culture. He became so zealous that his nextdoor neighbor, D. H. Lawrence, feared that he would destroy the Indians by "setting the claws of his own egotistic benevolent volition into them."[12]

At Taos, Collier found answers to the questions that had vexed him in his pursuit of urban reform in New York and California. He saw that Pueblo culture must survive not only in justice to the Indian but also in service to the white man. He realized that the Pueblos' integrated social organizations offered an example of community life to replace the fragmented world created by the Industrial Revolution. They possessed the lost attribute of communal and cooperative experience—the profound sense of living to be found in primary social groups. These Indians had discovered a way to be communalists and individualists at the same time.[13]

Collier realized that in New Mexico he had found a solution to the problem of whether materialism and selfish individualism would dominate and destroy man. He believed that Pueblo culture offered a model for the redemption of American society because it concerned itself very little with the material aspects of life. Instead, its goals were beauty, adventure, joy, comradeship, and the relationship of man to God. These Indians also held the secrets of social education and personality formation desperately needed by a more sophisticated white world.[14]

The vision that Collier experienced at Taos dramatically changed his life. Beginning in 1922, he severed former profes-

---

[12] Diana Trilling, *The Selected Letters of D. H. Lawrence* (New York: Farrar, Straus and Cudahy, 1958), p. 211; and Edward Nehls, ed., *D. H. Lawrence: A Composite Biography, 1919–1925*, 3 vols. (Madison: University of Wisconsin Press, 1957–1959), I: 197–199, 487.

[13] John Collier, "The Red Atlantis," *Survey*, October 1, 1922, p. 16; Collier, "The Pueblo's Last Stand," *Sunset*, February, 1923, p. 19; and Collier, "Plundering the Pueblo Indians," *Sunset*, January, 1923, p. 21.

[14] John Collier, "Our Indian Policy," *Sunset*, March, 1923, p. 13.

sional associations and launched a crusade against the forces attempting to crush Indian culture. Aware of the significance that the red man held for America, Collier, in the decade that preceded the New Deal, became the focus of demands for reform in the administration of Indian affairs.

Collier's career as critic of the Indian Bureau began with the General Federation of Women's Clubs, where, as research agent for its Indian Welfare Committee, he helped the Pueblo Indians organize resistance to the Bursum bill. Sponsored by Secretary of the Interior Albert B. Fall, this bill would have deprived the Indians of at least sixty thousand acres of disputed land. Its defeat helped preserve Pueblo life and had an impact on Fall's decision to resign from the Harding cabinet. More important, the defeat of the Bursum bill led to the formation, in 1923, of the American Indian Defense Association.[15]

Led by Collier, its executive secretary, the Defense Association had a membership of seventeen hundred persons and spent about $22,000 a year for legal-aid services.[16] Its program called for an investigation and reorganization of the Indian Bureau. It opposed the Dawes Severalty Act of 1887, which had dissipated Indian land and encouraged the rapid assimilation of the Indian into American society. Instead, the Association suggested that the trust period be extended on all allotted lands and the mineral resources of the reservations be placed in Indian hands, in order to make the tribes self-supporting, self-reliant, and prosperous.[17]

The preservation of Indian civilization became one of the most important objectives of Collier's Association. The Association

[15] Kenneth Philp, "Albert Fall and the Protest from the Pueblos, 1921–1923," *Arizona and the West* 12 (Autumn, 1970): 237–254.

[16] U.S., Congress, *Congressional Record*, 72nd Cong., 1st sess., March 10, 1932, 75, p. 5:5677.

[17] "Announcement of the Purpose of the American Indian Defense Association" (Collier Papers [n.d., but published 1923]).

proposed that Indian education develop rather than suppress group loyalties. It insisted that Indians have religious and social freedom in all matters where such freedom was not directly contrary to public morals. It recommended that Congress pass a statute ensuring religious liberty for all Indians, and it advocated that churches have the opportunity to convert, but not coerce, the Indians to Christianity.[18]

Under the influence of Collier, who worked as a lobbyist in Washington, D.C., the Defense Association made the 1920's a seedtime for reform in Indian affairs. The Association prevented the Indian Bureau, determined to turn the Indian into a white man, from suppressing Pueblo Indian religious dances and tribal self-government. Collier and his associates also prevented the confiscation of Indian oil and water-power sites on the Navajo and Flathead Indian reservations.[19] They helped start, in 1927, a Senate investigation of the Indian Bureau's work on the reservations, which exposed such inhuman conditions as the chaining of Indian children to their beds, at boarding schools, in order to prevent them from running back to their parents.[20] Finally, they offered several legislative alternatives, such as the Indian arts and crafts bill, which would become the basis for reforms enacted during the New Deal.[21]

President Franklin D. Roosevelt's appointment of Collier as Commissioner of Indian Affairs was a dramatic move to improve the status of one of America's neglected minority groups, and

[18] Ibid.
[19] John Collier, "Highlights of the Case for Removing Herbert Hagerman from the Government Payroll," February 29, 1932 (Collier Papers); Collier, "Monopoly in Montana," *The New Freeman*, May 3, 1930, pp. 1–2.
[20] John Collier, "Senators and Indians," *Survey Graphic*, January 1, 1929, pp. 425–426.
[21] John Collier, "The Immediate Tasks of the American Indian Defense Association," December 10, 1929 (Collier Papers).

Collier immediately embarked on a radical program to assist the American Indian. During a speech to the Navajo students at Fort Wingate in July, 1933, the new commissioner expressed the purpose of his Indian New Deal. First, he said that the government had the duty to bring education and modern scientific knowledge within the reach of every Indian. And, at the same time, the government should reawaken in the soul of the Indian not only pride in being an Indian, but also hope for his future as an Indian. It had the obligation to preserve the Indian's love of and ardor toward the rich values of Indian life as expressed in their arts, rituals, and cooperative institutions. Collier warned the Navajos, however, that if they turned away in scorn and shame from their heritage, they would not only be throwing away that part of their being which made them powerful and interesting as individuals, but they would also be canceling great spiritual contributions required in the future by American civilization.[22]

Because he was aware of the value that Indian culture held for the white world, Collier used his executive power to begin a fundamental change in the policies of the Indian Bureau. On May 25, 1933, Secretary of the Interior Harold Ickes, with Collier's approval, abolished the Board of Indian Commissioners. In its place, at Collier's request, Ickes created a consultant group of social scientists informed on the subject of Indian affairs. This group made up an Indian Bureau brain trust to advise the commissioner on such matters as Indian arts and crafts, cultural anthropology, education, use of natural resources, and law.[23]

[22] John Collier, "Talk to the Returned Students of the Navajos at Fort Wingate, New Mexico," July 7, 1933, National Archives, Record Group 316, Private Papers of Herbert Hagerman, Series I, Item 49, File on the Wheeler-Howard bill.

[23] Harold Ickes, memorandum for Commissioner Collier, July 29, 1933 (Collier Papers).

Collier's most controversial effort to protect Indian culture consisted of two executive orders that limited the influence of missionaries over Indian education and spiritual life. These orders represented the anticlerical thinking which permeated much of the Indian New Deal. The first order, dated January 3, 1934, was entitled "Indian Religious Freedom and Indian Culture." It demanded that "the fullest constitutional liberty, in all matters affecting religion, conscience and culture" exist for all Indians. In addition, it indicated that an "appropriate attitude" toward Indian heritage was desired in the Indian Service.[24]

The second order, dated January 15, 1934, curtailed missionary activity at Indian boarding schools. It prohibited compulsory attendance at religious services, but allowed any denomination, including representatives of a native Indian religion, to use the facilities at the boarding school for religious instruction, on condition that the children's attendance was by personal or parental choice.[25]

This second order also limited religious exercises at Indian day schools. Any child, however, upon the written request of his parents, might be excused for religious training, including instruction in a native Indian religion, for one hour each week. Furthermore, the day school facilities would be loaned for the use of denominational bodies only when not in use by the Indian Service or the community.[26]

These two resolutions struck at the heart of missionary work among the Indians. Activities in Oklahoma offer an example of the hostility manifested by many clergymen toward the Indian New Deal. Fearing that their religious work might be prohibited

24 John Collier, "Regulations for Religious Worship and Instruction," January 30, 1934, NA, RG 75, File on Religious Freedom.
25 Ibid.
26 Ibid.

among the Indians, two missionaries called a protest meeting on
November 1, 1934, at Oklahoma City. Over twenty missionaries,
representing twelve denominations, assembled at the Oklahoma
capital and adopted a resolution suggesting that Collier should
study the "pagan religions" to which he was encouraging the Indians to return.[27] In a separate statement, the Baptist General
Convention, which represented 185,000 white and Indian Bap-
tists, criticized any policy that would interfere with their work in
the government schools and support "the revival of such demoral-
izing ceremonial expressions as the use of peyote" by the Native
American Church.[28]

In an interview reported by the Associated Press, Collier criticized the "small minority" among the missionaries who were
agitating for the denial of liberty of conscience to Indians. He rejected the missionaries' demand that the Indian Bureau use official coercion to force Indian children into denominational classes
even though their parents belonged to other faiths. He called
such a policy "an outrage upon human nature as well as an ex-
press violation of the Constitution."[29]

In a lengthy letter to the Oklahoma *Tushkahomman*, Collier
rejected the accusation that he was an infidel and atheist, hostile
to the Christian religion. He reminded the missionaries that liberty of conscience in America was never meant to be liberty only
for those who professed Christianity. Collier pointed out that the
Bureau favored a protective attitude toward native religions because they "had been forged out through thousands of years of
striving and endurance, and search for truth," and because they

[27] John Collier, memorandum for Secretary Ickes, November 2, 1934,
NA, RG 75, File on Adverse Propaganda.
[28] E. C. Routh to John Collier, November 21, 1934, NA, RG 75, File
on Religious Freedom.
[29] John Collier, interview given to the Associated Press representative,
November 2, 1934, NA, RG 75, File on Adverse Propaganda.

contained "deep beauty, spiritual guidance, consolation, and disciplinary power."[30]

The missionaries opposing the Indian New Deal who believed Collier was antireligious were misinformed. The commissioner expressed his interest in the spiritual rejuvenation of America when he told the Christianized Indian students at Bacone College in Oklahoma that "the light which streams from 2,000 years ago" was now kindled for Indians as well as for many other Americans. Collier called upon these students to bring their "native endowment to the renewal of religion" in the United States. He told them that "religious-mindedness"—one of the most universal and emphasized traits of the Indian race—was needed, because "religion has come to run thin" in the present-day white world.[31]

Collier's most spectacular attempt to preserve Indian heritage came in June, 1934, when he secured the passage of the Indian Reorganization Act, which rejected the traditional policy of assimilation and Americanization of the Indian in favor of a policy of cultural pluralism. The philosophy behind this act implied that, instead of a melting pot, America ought to represent a great pageant of peoples. Fundamentally, the Indian Reorganization Act consisted of a declaration by the government that the Indians as a self-contained racial group must have the opportunity to enrich American culture.[32]

Attempting to bring alive again the whole range of native values centering around the collective ownership of land, the IRA abandoned land allotment and prohibited the future sale of un-

[30] John Collier to Ben Dwight, February 19, 1936, NA, RG 75, File on Religious Freedom.
[31] John Collier, "Talk to the Students of Bacone College," March 22, 1934, NA, RG 16, Records of the Office of the Secretary of Agriculture.
[32] Laura Thompson, *Culture in Crisis: A Study of the Hopi Indians* (New York: Harper and Brothers, 1950), pp. 147–151.

allotted land to non-Indians. It also gave the secretary of the interior the power to restore to various tribes surplus land created by the Dawes Severalty Act and to initiate conservation measures on Indian land. Another section made available an annual appropriation of $2 million, enabling the government to consolidate and acquire approximately 3 million acres of land for several reservations.[33]

The renewal of Indian political structures destroyed by the Dawes Act paralleled this restoration of land. The IRA set up a system of home rule similar to municipal government, utilizing tribal councils as vehicles for economic and social progress. It permitted tribes to incorporate and to operate property of every description.[34]

Other provisions of the IRA encouraged Indian self-respect and responsibility. A revolving credit fund advanced over $4 million to the Indians between 1934 and 1938.[35] Special civil-service requirements also allowed Indians to hold more positions in the Bureau, and an annual appropriation of $250,000 provided tuition and scholarships for promising Indian students.[36]

Collier hoped that the IRA would enable the Indians to develop a cooperative society that was neither materially acquisitive nor clearly communal, one that would combine individual initiative with an even distribution of wealth. He believed that such a society could escape the doctrinal controversies and social upheavals that plagued other parts of the world. Such a social is-

[33] U.S., *Statutes at Large*, 48, June 18, 1934, pp. 984–988; also, Felix Cohen, *Handbook of Federal Indian Law* (Washington, D.C.: Government Printing Office, 1942), p. 86.

[34] *Statutes at Large*, 48, pp. 984–988; Cohen, *Handbook*, p. 86.

[35] John Collier, *Annual Report of the Secretary of the Interior: Report of the Commissioner of Indian Affairs* (Washington, D.C.: Government Printing Office, 1938), p. 250.

[36] Ibid., 1941, p. 439; and U.S., *Statutes at Large*, 48, June 18, 1934, pp. 984–988.

land, busy equipping itself with the technique of cooperative action, could serve as a model to harried America.[37]

Under the commissioner's guidance several Indian tribes developed prosperous cooperatives. The Jicarilla Apaches successfully managed their tribal trading post, while the Menominee Indians operated their lumber mill at a profit. Other Indian cooperatives marketed wild rice, berries, maple sugar, and fur. But their effect proved minimal as a model for white society.[38]

Collier supplemented the IRA with other reforms to revitalize the spiritual life of the Indian. He described them as an effort to "plow up the Indian soul, to make the Indian again the master of his own mind."[39] Under his direction, the Bureau encouraged the revival of ancient dances, in disuse for over fifty years. Older men and women started teaching the arts of pottery-making and weaving to their younger children once more. In 1936, the Department of the Interior established an Indian Arts and Crafts Board. Its purpose included the enlargement of the market for Indian arts and crafts, the improvement of methods of production, and the use of a government trademark to protect Indian-made goods from imitation.[40]

In 1937 the commissioner also reaffirmed the Indian's close spiritual bond with the land by issuing an order establishing twelve roadless areas consisting of 4,475,000 acres, and four wild areas aggregating 84,000 acres, on Indian reservations. He

[37] John Collier, "Mexico: A Challenge," *Progressive Education Magazine,* February, 1932, pp. 95–98; and Collier, *American Indian Life,* July, 1931, pp. 32–34.

[38] *New York Times,* December 5, 1939, p. 6; April 25, 1937, Section IV, p. 8; and January 28, 1934, Section IV, p. 7.

[39] Ibid., July 14, 1935, Section VIII, p. 10.

[40] John Collier, "Does the Government Welcome the Indian Arts?" *American Magazine of Art* (Supplement), 27, September, 1934, pp. 10–11; and "The Development of Indian Arts and Crafts," *Monthly Labor Review,* March, 1938, pp. 655–658.

pointed out that "almost everywhere they go the Indians encounter the competition and disturbance of the white race. Most of them desire some place which is all their own." The roadless and wilderness areas would enable "these tribes to maintain a retreat where they might escape from the constant contact with white men."[41]

In much the same spirit, Collier helped Robert Yellowtail, Superintendent of the Crow reservation in Montana, obtain seventy-seven buffalo from Yellowstone National Park.[42] Superintendent Yellowtail suggested that the aim behind this wildlife program consisted of preserving the buffalo from extinction, turning the reservation into a sportsman's paradise, and providing the tribe with an adequate meat supply.[43] Collier supported the program because it reaffirmed his policy which assumed that the Indians possessed a valuable culture of their own.[44]

During the years before World War II, the commissioner's vision of improved opportunity for the Indians expanded to include all of the Western Hemisphere. He dreamed of creating a Pan-Indian movement stretching from Alaska to South America. In 1938 he drafted a resolution, presented before the Eighth International Conference of the American Republics, which paved the way for the first Inter-American Conference on Indian Life, held at Patzcuaro, Mexico, for ten days during the spring of 1940.[45]

The delegates at Patzcuaro internationalized the goals of Col-

[41] U.S., Department of the Interior, *Forest Conservation on Lands Administered by the Department of the Interior*, Part 2, *Forestry on Indian Lands* (Washington, D.C.: Government Printing Office, 1940), pp. 84–85.

[42] *New York Times*, May 26, 1935, Section VII, p. 10.

[43] *Indians at Work* (U.S. Gov't. pamphlet), May 15, 1936, pp. 28–30.

[44] *New York Times*, May 26, 1935, Section VII, p. 10.

[45] John Collier to Elmer Thomas, February 28, 1940 (Collier Papers); and Collier, *Indians of the Americas*, pp. 172–175.

lier's Indian New Deal when they adopted seventy-two resolutions calling for the betterment of Indian life. Most of these recommendations stemmed from the experience of the United States' administration of Indian affairs during the 1930's. It was proposed that each American government have an agency to protect Indian culture and to concentrate on working with Indians in groups. These agencies were also supposed to utilize cooperative institutions for Indian betterment and to provide the Indians with needed land credit and technical assistance.[46]

Collier's most dramatic effort to revive an Indian identity throughout the Western Hemisphere occurred when the representatives at Patzcuaro created by treaty a permanent Inter-American Indian Institute as the official agency responsible for maintaining collaboration between the fourteen member American republics on matters affecting Indians. Collier served as president of its governing board until May, 1946. The Institute published two bilingual journals, the quarterly *America Indígena* and the bi-monthly *Boletín Indigenista*, which fostered the interchange of information on the policies and programs being developed throughout the hemisphere on behalf of the Indians.[47]

As World War II progressed, the commissioner's attention focused not only on the American Indian but also on the problems of dependent peoples throughout the world. On January 15, 1943, he wrote an unsuccessful memorandum to President Roosevelt suggesting the creation of a civilian training program responsible "for relief, rehabilitation, and the administration of occupied areas" in the Pacific Ocean.[48] Collier wanted the president to establish in the Department of the Interior an "Institute of

[46] John Collier, radio broadcast, "The Future of the American Indian," October 27, 1941 (Collier Papers).

[47] Ibid.

[48] John Collier, memorandum for the President, January 15, 1943 (Collier Papers).

Ethnic Democracy" to train colonial administrators in the art of democratic administration.[49] He believed that the United States was not prepared for the custody of the new islands and territories in Micronesia at the end of the war. He felt that the "colonial record" of the Indian Bureau during the New Deal offered an example of how to govern nonindustrial and illiterate peoples. It could serve as "a laboratory of ethnic relations" which might help solve the post-war problems facing the United States.[50]

On January 19, 1945, Collier submitted his resignation as Indian commissioner to the President. He explained to Roosevelt that "working under your leadership and that of Secretary Ickes through these twelve years has been the most stimulating, developing, and fulfilling experience of my entire life." In spite of this, he wanted to enter private life in order to do justice to the Pan-Indian movement and to work in the area of ethnic relations as it related to the creation of a stable post-war world. Collier also pointed out that the removal of the Indian Bureau to Chicago during the war had created "all but insurmountable difficulties and problems," and that denial of adequate funds by the House appropriations subcommittee had recently nullified excellent legislative programs.[51]

The President accepted Collier's resignation on January 22, 1945, but told the commissioner in a letter that the country would never forget his contribution to the progress and welfare of the American Indian. Roosevelt praised Collier for protecting the Indians' cultural values, religious freedom, and property rights. He suggested that if the Indians possessed greater self-

[49] John Collier and Saul K. Padover, "Institute of Ethnic Democracy," *Common Ground* 4 (Autumn, 1943): 3–7.

[50] John Collier, "United States Administration as a Laboratory of Ethnic Relations," *Social Research* 12 (September, 1945): 265–268.

[51] John Collier to Franklin Roosevelt, January 19, 1945, Franklin D. Roosevelt Library, File no. 6-C.

respect and a stronger feeling of solidarity with the rest of the country it was because "as Commissioner, you have really believed in the Sermon on the Mount, the Declaration of Independence, and the Constitution, and have done what you have to make these symbols by which to live."[52]

The New Deal bought time for the American Indians' physical and spiritual survival. Collier was satisfied that they had "turned from anticipated death to anticipated life, from fatalism to action, from inferiority to healthful pride."[53] He hoped that in the future "their exceedingly rich expressions in many art forms would increase and would influence profoundly the art forms and the sense of the beautiful, throughout the white race." Collier also believed that "their ancient, deep, universal love of the earth . . . would continue to draw to them in fellow sharing, all who are young, all who have youth in their souls."[54]

The question remains: Was Collier's effort to ensure the Indian's cultural independence successful? The answer is yes, even though the Eisenhower administration followed a disastrous program of terminating the government's guardianship policy toward the red man. As Vine Deloria, a noted Sioux author and militant leader, has pointed out, the sons and daughters of parents who were influenced by Collier's Indian New Deal increasingly demand to be consulted about the future formulation of government Indian policies.[55]

The formation of the Indian Youth Council in August, 1960, at Gallup, New Mexico, offers an example of this new militancy. Mel Thom and nine other Indian radicals, known as the Red

[52] Franklin Roosevelt to Commissioner Collier, January 22, 1945, FDRL, File no. 6-C.
[53] *Annual Report of the Secretary of the Interior* (1939), pp. 23–24.
[54] John Collier, radio broadcast, "The Future of the American Indian," October 27, 1941 (Collier Papers).
[55] *New York Times*, March 8, 1970, Section VI, p. 54.

Muslims, set up an organization to oppose the termination of federal trusteeship and to retain their Indian heritage. The Council's first direct action, in 1964, was to organize "fish-ins" in the state of Washington, to protest the abrogation of the Indians' special treaty rights to fish in such areas as the Nisqually River. The Council also published a militant newspaper entitled *Americans before Columbus*. Clyde Warrior, its editor, asked Indians to give up their "Uncle Tomahawk" past and become "angry young nationalists."[56]

This plea did not fall on deaf ears, for on November 9, 1969, a small group of native Americans, mainly from San Francisco State College, occupied Alcatraz Island, the former site of the federal prison in San Francisco Bay. Their stated purpose was to persuade the government to turn the island into a West Coast Indian cultural center and vocational school.[57]

Collier died at Taos, New Mexico, in 1968. But if he had been alive, he would have been in sympathy with the attempts of those Indians to inaugurate an Indian renaissance—for which he worked so eagerly between 1920 and 1945. He would have understood the message of a young Indian militant who explained:

You will forgive me if I tell you that my people were Americans for thousands of years before your people were. The question is not how you can Americanize us but how we can Americanize you. The first thing we want to teach you is that, in the American way of life, each man has respect for his brother's vision. Because each of us respected his brother's dream, we enjoyed freedom here while your people were busy killing and enslaving one another across the water. We have a hard trail ahead of us but we are not afraid of hard trails.[58]

[56] Stan Steiner, *The New Indians* (New York: Dell Publishing Co., 1968), pp. 39–72.

[57] Rupert Costo, "Alcatraz," *The Indian Historian* 3 (Winter, 1970): 4–12.

[58] "The Angry American Indian: Starting down the Protest Trail," *Time*, February 9, 1970, p. 20.

RADICALISM IN THE GREAT DEPRESSION

BY JOHN A. GARRATY

IN 1934 THE HUNGARIAN ECONOMIST Eugen Varga attempted to sum up his impressions of the state of the world in the midst of the Great Depression. Varga was writing in Moscow; since the fall of the short-lived Communist government in his native Hungary in 1920 he had been studying the economy of the capitalist world as an employee of the Comintern. Varga was, of course, a Communist, but he was too independent minded to parrot any particular line or dogma. "There is no 'left-wing' or 'right-wing' analysis," he had written in 1925. "There is no 'opportunist' or 'revolutionary' perspective. There is only a right and a wrong perspective . . . and a successful revolutionary policy can be built only upon an analysis based on facts." This independence of mind had cost Varga his position as chief economist for the Soviet Union, but it had not ended his work. In 1927 he had become director of a Moscow research organization, the Institute for World Economy and World Politics. The current economic situation, he wrote in 1934, was unprecedented, "a depression of a special kind, without any prospect of a new prosperity phase" had engulfed the capitalist world. "There is only one way out for the proletariat: the revolutionary overthrow of the rule of the bourgeoisie. . . . Never before has there been such a glut of commodities alongside the misery and starvation of the working-class masses. Never before has it been so clear that the capitalist system of society must be overthrown, if mankind is to live as men!"

Even earlier in the depression the procapitalist experts of the Economic Intelligence Service of the League of Nations, in a comprehensive economic survey of the period 1932–1933, confessed that "economic activity in the world as a whole had touched depths unprecedented during the present depression, and international economic organization was in a state of extreme confusion." The League economists compared the world collapse to "a landslide which carried with it buildings, fields, walls, and living objects. As the landslide continued, the more vulnerable of the buildings collapsed, and in collapsing, started a fresh downward movement."[1]

Just how bad things were all over the world in the 1930's is difficult for persons who did not live through the Great Depres-

---

[1] L. M. Tikos, "Waiting for the World Revolution: Soviet Reactions to the Great Depression," *Journal of Contemporary History* 4 (1969): 91–92; Eugen Varga, *The Great Crisis and Its Political Consequences* (New York: International Publishers, 1934), p. 9; League of Nations, *World Economic Survey: 1932–1933* (Geneva: League of Nations, 1933), pp. 11, 63. The conservative British economist Lionel Robbins wrote: "There have been many depressions in modern economic history but it is safe to say that there has never been anything to compare with this" (*The Great Depression* [New York: Macmillan, 1934], p. 11). As early as 1930, John Maynard Keynes called the depression "one of the greatest economic catastrophes of modern history" (*Essays in Persuasion* [New York: W. W. Norton, 1963], p. 135). Recalling the mood of the period, the post–World War II British Prime Minister Harold Macmillan wrote: "The structure of capitalist society in its old form had broken down. . . . Perhaps it could not survive at all; it certainly could not survive without radical change" (*Winds of Change* [New York: Harper and Row, 1966], p. 266).

sion to realize,[2] but easy to demonstrate both statistically and by reference to specific events. In 1933 the International Labor Office estimated world unemployment at 30 million. Two-thirds of this total were concentrated in the three leading industrial nations: over 13 million were Americans, almost 6 million Germans, 2.8 million Englishmen. But every nation suffered greatly and the ranks of the jobless were increasing steadily nearly everywhere.[3] The world output of industrial products, according to separate studies by the League of Nations and the highly regarded German Institute for Business-Cycle Research, fell by about 25 per cent between 1929 and 1932. Prices plummeted—those of raw materials by over 60 per cent. Between January, 1929, and June, 1933, the gold value of world trade fell from almost $5.4 billion to $1.8 billion.

The collapse in the Western industrial nations was catastrophic. Between 1929 and 1932, industrial output in both the United States and Germany fell by 47 per cent, by 36 per cent in Czechoslovakia, 31 per cent in Belgium, 16 per cent in England and the Netherlands. In France, where the decline was less precipitous, it lasted longer; as late as 1935 it approached 30 per cent. Yet in many respects the underdeveloped nations suffered still more, since the prices of agricultural products and other raw materials fell more sharply than those of manufactured goods.[4]

[2] The special concern of historians of the depression with the problem of re-creating the atmosphere of the times is discussed in Bernard Sternsher, ed., *Hitting Home: The Great Depression in Town and Country* (Chicago: Quadrangle Books, 1970), pp. 3–6.

[3] League of Nations, *Economic Survey, 1932–1933*, pp. 32–33, 109. Between 1929 and 1933, for example, unemployment increased from 39,000 to 109,000 in Australia, from 28,000 to 383,000 in Belgium, from 50,000 to 787,000 in Czechoslovakia, from 9,000 to 113,000 in Switzerland. All these figures are probably too low, for the tendency was to underrepresent agricultural and part-time unemployment.

[4] Ibid., pp. 9, 32–33, 54–61, 71; Alfred Sauvy, *Histoire économique de la France entre les deux guerres* (Paris: Fayard, 1967) II, 139, 142;

The impact of this Great Depression on individual human beings was equally profound and pervasive. Contemporary evidence of this is overwhelming; there is time here only to cite a few examples. In our own country, *Fortune* magazine (certainly no radical organ) generalized about the plight of the jobless in the summer of 1932:

You are a carpenter. Your last cent is gone. They have cut off the gas. The kid is white and stupid looking. . . . You can't get a job now for love or money. What do you do? In some, but by no means all cities you can get a meal at the Salvation Army. . . . But that's no use now. So you go to a cop. He pulls out his directory and sends you to one of the listed charitable societies. . . . You draw the Episcopal Relief Society. The Relief Society clears your name through the central agency to see that you are not receiving help elsewhere. Eventually [it will] allot you $2 to $8 a week, depending on the locality and the funds available. If its funds are exhausted it asks you to wait.

Fortune's article was entitled "No One Has Starved," but, as the editors admitted, this was not entirely true. Numerous deaths directly attributable to malnutrition were reported in the newspapers; as early as 1931 four New York City hospitals treated ninety-five cases of starvation in a single year, and twenty of these patients died. For some unfortunates, jail was a form of relief society. Here is an item from the *New York Times* of October 7, 1932:

Fifty-four men were arrested yesterday morning for sleeping or idling in the arcade connecting with the subway through 45 W. 42 Street, but most of them considered their unexpected meeting with a raiding party of ten policemen as a stroke of luck because it brought them free meals yesterday and shelter last night from the sudden change of the weather.

William Arthur Lewis, *Economic Survey: 1919–1939* (New York: Harper and Row, 1969), p. 61.

And here is Malcolm X's recollection of growing up in the thirties in East Lansing, Michigan:

. . . by 1934, we really began to suffer. This was about the worst depression year, and no one we knew had enough to eat or live on. Some old family friends visited us now and then. At first they brought food. Though it was charity, my mother took it. . . . In Lansing, there was a bakery where, for a nickel, a couple of us children would buy a tall flour sack of day-old bread and cookies, and then walk two miles back into the country to our house. . . . But there were times when there wasn't even a nickel and we would be so hungry we were dizzy. My mother would boil a big pot of dandelion greens and we would eat that.[5]

In England unemployment had been a chronic problem throughout the twenties and social services were better organized than in America. Nevertheless, conditions for many of the poor in the depression became almost unbearable. In 1936 the Pilgrim Trust, a philanthropic organization, sponsored an investigation of the problem, directed by the Bishop of York. After studying 1,086 sample cases, the Trust concluded, for example, that "the low material standard allowed for a large family by the present assistance rates means that in few families with four or more children is it possible to maintain the equipment of the household, renew shoes and clothes and also buy sufficient food." Of eighty unemployed families in Liverpool, investigators discovered that in about one-third of the cases the mother was suffering from ane-

---

[5] *Fortune*, September, 1932, pp. 19, 22; Harris Warren, *Herbert Hoover and the Great Depression* (New York: Oxford University Press, 1959), p. 199; Irving Bernstein, *The Lean Years: A History of the American Worker, 1920–1933* (Baltimore: Penguin Books, 1966), p. 331; *New York Times*, October 7, 1932, quoted in D. A. Shannon, ed., *The Great Depression* (Englewood Cliffs: Prentice Hall, 1960), p. 13; Malcolm Little, *The Autobiography of Malcolm X* (New York: Grove Press, 1966, paperback ed.), p. 13.

mia, psychological disturbances, or some other form of illness. Here is what the Trust reported about one family:

... there were seven children, the parents' ages being 36 and 32. The allowance was 43s. 6d., and we reckoned the value of milk from the clinic and of free milk in school for two of the children at an extra 2s. With 8s. rent, this left 37s. 6d. available as against 52s. 1d. required by our "poverty" standard. The man was physically a very fine type, and was active-minded and intelligent. . . . Though the house was not particularly dirty, it was not clean, the furniture was meagre and in pieces, the clothes of all of them very ragged, and the general impression given was that any attempt to maintain standards in such matters had been abandoned as hopeless. . . . It seemed that the family . . . had not lost the consciousness of the standards that might be maintained, but that they had given up struggling to maintain them in the home. There is obviously a vicious circle, for when the task once gets beyond them, the effort to carry it through becomes progressively more ineffective.

In 1933, the English novelist J. B. Priestley reported attending a reunion of his World War battalion in Bradford, his home town. When he noticed that several of the veterans of his platoon were not present even though he and some of the others had arranged to pay the cost of their dinners, he was told that "they were so poor, these fellows, that they said they could not attend the dinner even if provided with free tickets because they felt that their clothes were not good enough. . . . We could drink to the tragedy of the dead; but we could only stare at one another, in pitiful embarrassment, over this tragi-comedy of the living, who had fought for a world that did not want them, who had come back to exchange their uniforms for rags."[6]

[6] *Men Without Work: A Report Made to the Pilgrim Trust*, with an Introduction by the Archbishop of York and a Preface by Lord Macmillan (Cambridge, England: The University Press, 1938), pp.

In France, where the franc was worth less than five cents, hourly wages of eighty centimes were not uncommon, and, in 1936, more than 3.6 million of the *employed* earned less than the equivalent of $500 a year. Working conditions were terrible. As René Duchemin, powerful president of the Confédération Générale de la Production Française, later put it: "How could we have let it happen? We failed in our duty by letting things get like that." The French city of Besançon, an important center of watch manufacturing with a population of 58,000, reported in June, 1932, that nine out of every ten watchmakers were either totally unemployed or working sharply reduced hours. The municipal authorities, the local church, the army, and, of course, many private citizens struggled to aid the unfortunates, setting up soup kitchens for the hungry and dormitories for the homeless, and providing direct financial aid. Yet, as the historian of the crisis in Besançon concludes, "in spite of all, this aid was insufficient to prevent impoverishment."[7]

In the Austrian town of Marienthal, where the closing of the local textile factory put virtually the whole community out of work, an investigator reported as follows about a family of four, a mother and three children: "There is no money for anything but milk and bread. It takes 10 schillings to pay for milk for 14 days, for food and coal about 40. The few remaining schillings go for incidentals. One can't buy anything else. The little seven-year-

---

116, 127, 128–130; J. B. Priestley, *English Journey* (New York: Harper and Brothers, 1934), p. 136.

[7] J. Touchard and L. Bodin, "L'état de l'opinion au début de l'année 1936," in J. Boudin, ed., *Léon Blum, chef de gouvernement, 1936–1937* (Paris: Colin, 1967), p. 53; Simone Weil, *La Condition ouvrière* (Paris: Gallimard, 1951), pp. 35–108; M. Daclin, *La Crise des années 30 à Besançon*, Cahiers d'Etudes Comptoises 13, Annales Littéraires de l'Université de Besançon, vol. 96 (Paris: Les Belles Lettres, 1968), pp. 79, 89–92, 119.

old had to stay home from school for a week because he had no
shoes."[8]

Unemployment was most serious in Germany. Some of its de-
plorable by-products were reported in 1931 by the Prussian welfare ministry: "For children unemployment causes undernourish-
ment, increasing illness and [parental] indifference to their
hygienic needs. . . . Very often the doctor is called too late or not at
all because the necessary fees are not available. . . . Children frequently fall ill in school because of anemia and hunger. Cases of
dizziness and fainting are rising sharply, even among older children." Similar reports exist in profusion, but perhaps the impres-
sionistic observations of contemporaries are more revealing. After visiting a dozen Berlin bars frequented by unemployed men in
1932, the writer H. R. Knickerbocker noted that only about one
man in ten had a glass of beer in front of him. "If a German is
so poor that he cannot buy a beer, he has reached the point of
despair," Knickerbocker wrote. Annual beer consumption, he
discovered, was down from 102.1 liters per capita in 1913 to
74.7 liters in 1931. And the archeologist Ludwig Curtius, who
frequently traveled outside Germany by auto during the depression, recalled in his autobiography that he often picked up young
Germans on the road, sometimes treating them to a meal. "No
more did mere *Wanderlust* drive them to foreign lands," he
wrote, "but necessity." Purposelessly they wandered, deprived,
living off the kindness of foreigners. Their stories were all substantially the same—parents and older brothers unemployed, sav-
ings lost, education no longer possible. "What could I say to
them?" Curtius asked.[9]

Such widespread misery and deprivation led to protests, to de-

[8] Marie Jahoda, et al., *Die Arbeitslosen von Marienthal* ([Allens-
bach] Verlag für Demoskopie, [1960], p. 34. This is a reprint of the
Leipzig edition, 1933.

[9] Wilhelm Treue, ed., *Deutschland in der Weltwirtschaftskrise in*

mands for radical action, and to violence, when nothing—or not enough—was done about the situation. In Great Britain, where high unemployment long antedated the world depression, protest meetings, Communist-led hunger marches, and disorganized rioting occurred sporadically. There had been a general strike as early as 1926. In September, 1931, the sailors of the Atlantic Fleet based at Invergordon mutinied in protest against a pay cut. The communist National Unemployed Workers' Movement repeatedly agitated for greater relief for the jobless, attracting much middle-class sympathy both through their ragged demonstrations and because of the brutal way the demonstrations were often broken up by the police. After one great riot in Birkenhead in 1932, thirty-seven policemen and over one hundred demonstrators were hospitalized.[10]

Similar outbursts occurred in the United States. The famous march on Washington of the Bonus Army in 1932 was but the most spectacular of the American protests. The historian Bernard Sternsher has put together a list of seventeen incidents of violent protest between February, 1930, and July, 1932, which he admits is "just a sampling." After three persons were killed during anti-eviction demonstrations in Chicago in 1931, for example, sixty thousand people participated in a funeral march to protest the police violence. On International Unemployment Day (March 6, 1930) great crowds gathered in many cities; fighting with the police erupted repeatedly.[11]

Augenzeugenberichten (Düsseldorf: Rauch, 1967), pp. 248, 348–349, 337–338.

[10] Walter Hannington, *Unemployed Struggles: 1919–1936* (London: Lawrence and Wishart, 1936), pp. 234–235 and passim; A. J. P. Taylor, *English History: 1914–1944* (New York and London: Oxford University Press, 1970), pp. 372, 433; Robert Graves and Alan Hodge, *The Long Weekend: A Social History of Great Britain* (New York: W. W. Norton, 1963), pp. 258–259, 333.

[11] Sternsher, *Hitting Home*, p. 10; Richard Hofstadter and M. Wal-

Widespread disorders took place also in rural areas. During the summer of 1932, the so-called Farmers' Holiday Association staged a milk strike in Iowa in protest against low milk prices. Throwing a cordon around Sioux City, strikers stopped milk trucks on the highways, sometimes dumping their contents on the roadside. When pickets were arrested, mobs forced their release, and the angry farmers also prevented foreclosure sales by mass action and intimidation. In 1933 and 1934, about 100 agricultural strikes, involving over 87,000 laborers, occurred in the nation. Workers in the cranberry bogs of Massachusetts, apple pickers in Washington, and migrant labor groups in California, among others, took militant action against their dreadful lot, despite brutal repression by local authorities.

Beyond such large-scale confrontations were countless smaller examples of violence, often ignored by authorities and the press. John Dos Passos, writing in the *New Republic* in 1932, reported an incident of this type in Detroit. A group of men entered a large food store and asked for credit. When told the store sold only for cash, they forced the clerks to stand aside and took what they needed from the shelves. The manager did not call the police. "If more people heard about affairs like this," he told Dos Passos, "there would be more trouble."[12]

---

lace, eds., *American Violence: A Documentary History* (New York: Alfred A. Knopf, 1970), pp. 172–175; A. M. Schlesinger, Jr., *The Crisis of the Old Order, 1919–33* (Boston: Houghton Mifflin, 1957), p. 167; Saul Wellman, "A Memoir of the Thirties," in *The Great Depression: Essays and Memoirs from Canada and the United States*, edited by Victor Hoar (Vancouver: Copp Clark Publishing Co., 1969), pp. 157–158.

[12] J. L. Shover, "The Farmers' Holiday Association Strike, August, 1932," *Agricultural History* 39 (1965): 196–203; Irving Bernstein, *Turbulent Years* (Boston: Houghton Mifflin, 1970), pp. 142–170; Matthew Josephson, *Infidel in the Temple* (New York: Alfred A. Knopf, 1967), p. 96.

In Germany, the social disintegration of the early 1930's, which contributed to the Nazi seizure of power in 1933, was not entirely a result of the depression. It is often difficult to distinguish the purely political violence of Nazi storm troopers from disorders rising out of poverty and unemployment. The Nazis' efforts to capitalize on working-class dissatisfaction—as early as 1928 they published a propaganda sheet, *Der Erwerblose* (The Unemployed)—were not very successful. But many Germans became Nazis either because of the direct threat of the depression or because of the violent responses to economic problems of radical workers and ultraconservative peasants. Hunger marches, demands for "bread and work," mass protests in great cities and small towns, during which desperate unemployed men threatened to hang local officials, increased in frequency as the depression worsened. In December, 1932, hundreds of men and women in the city of Halle forced a terrified fuel dealer to give them free coal, which they carted away by the wagonload.[13]

French disorders during the depression were also partly political. The rightist-led Paris riots of February 6, 1934, for example, were probably triggered by reactionaries' fears of communism and by exasperation with the instability and ineffectuality of the French parliament—there had been five changes of government in the past eighteen months. Similarly, the general strike that followed was essentially a protest against French fascism, not against economic conditions. But, as in Gemany, the depression greatly exacerbated political conflicts in France. The economic discontent erupted most dramatically in the great wave of sitdown strikes which swept the country in the spring of 1936. Over a million workers—factory hands, construction workers, even department-

[13] Karl D. Bracher, *The German Dictatorship* (New York: Praeger, 1970), pp. 154–157; William S. Allen, *The Nazi Seizure of Power: The Experience of a Single German Town* (London: Eyre and Spottiswood, 1966), pp. 154, 116–117; Treue, *Weltwirtshaftskrise*, p. 346.

store clerks—occupied nearly nine thousand places of employment by force and refused to leave until their demands were met. Their frightened employers, pressed by the government, yielded within a matter of days, and a minor socioeconomic revolution resulted.[14]

The protests of the poor and their suffering moved many intellectuals deeply, with the result that there was a massive outpouring of radical literature. This was particularly true in the United States, where many intellectuals had moved leftward even in the prosperous twenties, impelled by the arch-conservative, pro-business policies of the Harding-Coolidge era. To say that, as one of them recently claimed, "almost every American writer worth his salt in the thirties either flirted with or was married to or had a clandestine affair with the Communist Party sometime between 1929 and 1939," is something of an overstatement, but many writers were indeed party members and still more were extremely critical of American society. John Steinbeck's *Grapes of Wrath* and John Dos Passos's *U.S.A.* are among the best remembered of a flood of American depression novels.[15] *Love on the Dole*, by

[14] Max Beloff, "The 6th of February," in *The Decline of the Third Republic*, edited by James Joll (London: Chatto and Windus, 1959), pp. 13–15; James Joll, "Making of the Popular Front," in ibid., p. 41; Joel Colton, *Léon Blum: Humanist in Politics* (New York: Alfred A. Knopf, 1966), p. 99; Antoine Prost, "Les Grèves de juin 1936," in *Léon Blum, chef de gouvernement, 1936–1937*, pp. 69–87; Georges Lefranc, *Histoire du front populaire (1934–1938)* (Paris: Payot, 1965), pp. 137–156. For interesting accounts of the sitdowns by strikers themselves, see Georges Lefranc, *Juin 36: L'Explosion sociale* (Paris: Julliard, 1966), pp. 181–222.

[15] Kenneth Ledbetter, "Marxism and American Literature," in Hoar, *Great Depression*, p. 116. See also Daniel Aaron, *Writers on the Left: Episodes in American Literary Communism* (New York: Harcourt, Brace & World, 1961), pp. 149 ff.; Harvey Swados, ed., *The American Writer and the Great Depression* (Indianapolis: Bobbs-Merrill, 1966), provides a convenient sampling of depression literature. For the attitude of English intellectuals and writers, see, for example, Victor

the English proletarian novelist Walter Greenwood, is in the same tradition, as are Hans Fallada's *Little Man, What Now?*, an account of the economic decline of a decent, hardworking, young German couple in Berlin, and Bertolt Brecht's stage classic, the *Dreigroschenoper*, or *Threepenny Opera*, in which Brecht's Mackie the Knife taunts the German bourgeoisie with the warning that their apparently docile, law-abiding workers would no longer tolerate starvation. "First comes feeding one's face, then comes morality," Brecht insisted.

"There is a crime here that goes beyond denunciation," Steinbeck wrote. "There is a sorrow here that weeping cannot symbolize. There is a failure here that topples all our success. . . . In the souls of the people the grapes of wrath are filling and growing heavy, growing heavy for the vintage." And thus Fallada: "How could one laugh, really laugh in such a world as this, a world of respectable and blundering captains of industry and little degraded down-trodden people always trying to do their best? . . . Order and cleanliness; they were of the past. So too were work and safe subsistence. And so too were progress and hope. Poverty was not merely misery, poverty was an offense, poverty was evil, poverty meant that a man was suspect."[16]

Gollancz, *Reminiscences of Affection* (New York: Atheneum, 1968), pp. 100–101; and Storm Jameson, *Journey from the North* (New York: Harper and Row, 1970), pp. 293–299.

[16] Peter Gay, *Weimar Culture: The Outsider as Insider* (New York: Harper and Row, 1968), p. 138; John Steinbeck, *The Grapes of Wrath* (New York: Viking Press, 1939), p. 378; Rudolf Ditzen, *Little Man, What Now?* by Hans Fallada [pseud.] (New York: Simon and Schuster, 1933), pp. 319, 370. All these fictional assaults on depression conditions were extremely popular. Brecht converted the *Threepenny Opera* into a novel and a film; *Little Man, What Now?* was a best seller. Walter Greenwood's *Love on the Dole* (London: Cape, 1933) was adapted for the stage by Ronald Gow and ran successfully in New York and London and, as *Rêves sans provision*, in Paris *(La Petite Illustration*, no. 418, June 26, 1937, p. 27). Fiction of this type was

Many writers also spoke out directly in works of nonfiction. Priestley, never a Communist, denounced the status quo in scalding terms in *English Journey*. After describing a conversation with a bankrupt tycoon, he wrote: "I do not blame him in particular, I blame us all for allowing such a daft chaos to go blundering on." He visited a hostel for the jobless, where idle young men played Ping-Pong by the hour. "Many of these unemployed lads . . . are very good at table tennis," he noted. "Probably, by the time the North of England is an industrial ruin, we shall be able to beat the world at table tennis." In America, James Agee movingly portrayed the hopeless poverty of rural America in *Let Us Now Praise Famous Men* (1941), and Theodore Dreiser, Sherwood Anderson, and Erskine Caldwell are only some of the most important American novelists who wrote books denouncing the evils of the depression.[17]

Social critics in all nations thundered against the "system," and their books frequently achieved enormous popularity. John Strachey's *The Coming Struggle for Power* (1932), a persuasive argument for a Marxist society, is an outstanding English example. By 1937 the Left Book Club in Great Britain, which published

uncommon in France. A so-called proletarian school existed, but its members concentrated on rather romanticized descriptions of the feelings and life styles of common workers, not on economic conditions per se. Most French novels of social criticism in the thirties dealt with earlier times. See, for example, Louis Aragon's *Les Cloches de Bâle* (1934) and *Les Beaux quartiers* (1936); both deal with the period before World War I. On French proletarian writers, see Henry Poulaille, *Nouvel âge littéraire* (Paris: Valois, 1930), pp. 221–438.

[17] Priestley, *English Journey*, pp. 161, 224; James Agee and Walker Evans, *Let Us Now Praise Famous Men* (Boston: Houghton Mifflin, 1944); Theodore Dreiser, *Tragic America* (New York: Liveright, 1931); Sherwood Anderson, *Puzzled Americans* (New York: Charles Scribner's Sons, 1935); Erskine Caldwell, *Some American People* (New York: R. M. McBride, 1935).

many works by radicals, had enrolled forty thousand members.[18]

The enormous disparity between the conditions of life for the rich and for the poor in bad times particularly outraged critics elsewhere. In France, writers denounced the "200 Families" that dominated not only business and finance, but also the press and the higher civil service. Augustin Hamon's *Masters of France* spelled out in italicized detail the network of business and family connections uniting these oligarchs. Among bankers, insurance executives, newspaper publishers, government administrators, and members of Parliament, Hamon concluded, "the intermixture of families one with the other is the same. The intermixture is so deep and so extensive that almost everyone is related to everyone else. It is the same as in a village isolated from the world, where the inhabitants marry among themselves." The "Upper Hundred" magnates of German capitalism were subjected to a similar, though briefer analysis in Ferdinand Fried's *The End of Capitalism*, which also denounced the maldistribution of wealth in a supposedly democratic society. "In Germany, 80,000 persons possess twice as much wealth as 62.5 million!" Fried exclaimed. He compared the lot of a poor family, where "five persons live in a tiny whitewashed room, no one having a bed to himself, eating grits and potato soup," with that of the "plutocracy who ape the formality of the old nobility, build themselves costly country seats, travel for the season to Baden-Baden, and would gladly let

[18] Graves, *Long Weekend*, pp. 333–334; Noreen Branson and Margot Heinemann, *Britain in the Nineteen Thirties* (London: Weidenfeld and Nicolson, 171), pp. 275–278. The Left Book Club was controlled by Strachey, Harold Laski, and the publisher, Victor Gollancz, all Marxists. In addition to publishing books, the club organized lectures and ran a theater group. A Labour Book Club and a Socialist Book Club in Britain were less successful. Strachey, who wrote *The Coming Struggle for Power* in America, became a successful lecturer in the United States during the depression (Josephson, *Infidel*, p. 315).

themselves be called Kaisers, Kings, or Princes of their businesses
—coal barons!" The Krupps, with assets of 200 million marks,
mostly in heavy industry, the family of Prince zu Hohenlohe-
Oehringen, with a fortune valued at 100 million marks invested
in land, mines, and housing, and dozens of other German tycoons felt the sting of Fried's lash. The Upper Hundred, he concluded, "or more exactly 110 rich individuals or families . . . own
altogether property worth about 3.4 billion marks."[19]

In the United States, where the muckraking tradition was well
established long before the depression and where great concentra-
tions of wealth were popularly considered threats to political democracy and economic free enterprise even in good times, radical
assaults of this type also flourished. Gustavus Myers's early-twen-
tieth-century *History of the Great American Fortunes*, prototype
of these attacks, was reissued by the mass-circulation Modern Library in the mid-thirties. Ferdinand Lundberg's *America's 60
Families* (1936) and Matthew Josephson's *The Robber Barons*
(1934) were best sellers. The spirit of these works is well ren-
dered in the concluding lines of *The Robber Barons*:

Soon there would be few who hoped that the old economic rulership
. . . could minister to the just needs of the masses of citizens, the
workers in the mills, the tillers of the land. . . . And during the long
years of industrial lethargy, while grass literally grew upon the floors
of magnificent factories, the lesson would finally be driven home of
the fearful sabotage practiced by capital upon the energy and intelligence of human society. . . . When the busy workers of our cities
were turned into idle and hungry louts, and our once patriotic farmers into rebels and lawbreakers, there would arise hosts of men and

[19] Augustin Hamon, *Les Maîtres de la France*, 3 vols. (Paris: Edi-
tions Sociales Internationales, 1936–1938) II, 341; Friedrich Zimmer-
man [Ferdinand Fried, pseud.], *Das Ende des Kapitalismus* (Jena: E.
Diederichs, 1931), pp. 62–81. See also Gaëtan Pirou, *La Crise du
capitalisme* (Paris: Recueil Sirey, 1933), p. 106.

women, numerous enough, who knew that "they could no longer live in a world where such things can be."[20]

Still another spur to radicalism in the industrial nations was the widespread failure of political "establishments" to react promptly and intelligently to the hardships the crisis was causing so many millions. President Hoover in the United States, Chancellors Hermann Müller and Heinrich Brüning in Germany (the one a Socialist, the other somewhat to the right of the middle of the road), Prime Minister Ramsay MacDonald in Great Britain, and a parade of French premiers—Herriot, Daladier, Doumergue, Laval, among others—failed to provide real leadership in the battle to restore economic equilibrium, or even to provide adequate relief for their suffering people.

Just as, when syphilis first became a serious disease in Europe in the late fifteenth century, the French called it "the Italian disease," the English "the French pox," the Poles "the German sickness," and so on, so nearly all the politicians tried to blame the social disease of the 1930's on some other nation than their own. "The 'Great Depression' did not start in the United States," Herbert Hoover explained in his *Memoirs*. The "economic hurricane struck us from abroad." French leaders, in turn, blamed the depression either on the Americans, because of their abandonment of the gold standard and their "exporting" of unemployment, or on foreign workers in France, who were taking bread from hungry French mouths. The Germans, and by no means only the Nazis, charged that the depression was a result of the Carthaginian terms of the Versailles Treaty and the sudden cutting off of American loans. The British argued that *too much* American credit and the collapse of prices on the New York

[20] Matthew Josephson, *The Robber Barons: The Great American Capitalists, 1861–1901* (New York: Harcourt, Brace, 1934), pp. 452–453.

Stock Exchange lay at the root of the slump. Socialist leaders accused the capitalist system, old-fashioned conservatives the "meddling" of Socialists with the functioning of the free-market economy.[21]

Professional economists struggled to find solutions to the problems of the depression. They offered much bad advice and often disagreed violently among themselves, and they developed a comprehensive new theory of economic recovery only slowly. (John Maynard Keynes's *General Theory* was not published until 1936.) Nevertheless, as a group they suggested many practical ideas which knowledgeable persons believed merited at least a trial. These included some kind of inflation of national currencies and credit facilities to check the catastrophic decline of prices, public works programs to help reduce unemployment, expanded relief grants to aid the destitute, deficit financing to pay for these, and, in general, an expansion of government activity and regulation in economic affairs. Repeatedly the advice was ignored.[22]

The experiences of Keynes, by far the most original economist of the interwar period and a man with a gift for expressing complex ideas in nontechnical language, demonstrate the obtuseness of contemporary statesmen. In May, 1929, he wrote a pamphlet favoring a public works program in Britain. His plan was rejected.[23] When the Labour party prime minister, Ramsay MacDon-

[21] Herbert Hoover, *Memoirs: The Great Depression, 1929–1941* (New York: Macmillan, 1952), p. vi; Sauvy, *Histoire économique,* II, 362. The Socialist prime minister of Great Britain, Ramsay MacDonald, said: "*We* are not on trial; it is the system under which we live. . . . It has broken down everywhere, as it was bound to break down" (A. J. P. Taylor, *English History,* pp. 358–359). On the European reaction to syphilis, see Samuel Eliot Morison, *Admiral of the Ocean Sea: A Life of Columbus* (Boston: Little, Brown, 1942), II: 193–194.
[22] Joseph Dorfman, *The Economic Mind in American Civilization,* 5 vols. (New York: Viking Press, 1959), V, 772.
[23] Keynes, *Essays in Persuasion,* pp. 118–134; A. J. Youngson,

ald, appointed him to a committee of experts in 1930 to recommend an economic policy, he and the other members labored hard and long, "forced," as the historian Robert Skidelsky has put it, "by the pressure of facts to re-examine the whole basis of their beliefs in an effort to find remedies to meet a desperate situation." But their moderate proposals were turned down in favor of the "policy" of the Treasury department, a policy that had MacDonald's entire approval. The idea of reducing unemployment through public works was illusory, the Treasury held. The economy was like "a great ship which has run aground on a falling tide; no human endeavour will get the ship afloat until in the course of nature the tide again begins to flow." During these years Keynes clashed with nearly all the leading financial experts of British officialdom, including Montagu Norman, governor of the Bank of England, and Sir Richard Hopkins of the Treasury. He characterized MacDonald's 1931 budget as "replete with folly and injustice" and "a policy of Bedlam." When, late in 1931, he published a collection of his essays, he described them ruefully in his preface as "the croakings of a Cassandra who could never influence the course of events in time."[24]

The story of Keynes's attempts to educate Franklin Roosevelt, of whose New Deal policies he, in general, approved, is well known. He spoke with the President in Washington in June, 1934, apparently trying, among other things, to explain the

---

Britain's Economic Growth: 1922–1966 (New York: Kelley, 1966), pp. 294–295. Objecting to government spending at the present time, Keynes wrote, "is like warning a patient who is wasting away from emaciation of the dangers of excessive corpulence."

[24] Robert Skidelsky, *Politicians and the Slump: The Labour Government of 1929–31* (London: Macmillan, 1967), p. 217; Roy Forbes Harrod, *The Life of John Maynard Keynes* (London: Macmillan, 1951), pp. 418–422, 438; Andrew Boyle, *Montagu Norman: A Biography* (London: Cassell, 1967), pp. 255–257; Keynes, *Essays in Persuasion,* p. v.

"multiplier" effect of public works programs, but Roosevelt was only confused by what he called Keynes's "rigamarole of figures." And in 1938 the economist wrote a long and candid letter to the President full of shrewd advice on how to deal with the 1937–1938 recession. Again Roosevelt failed to appreciate his suggestions, and he sent Keynes no more than a routine acknowledgement, actually drafted by the conservative secretary of the treasury, Henry Morgenthau.[25]

In Germany, Keynes's work attracted considerable attention among economists in the early years of the depression, but his influence on pre-Hitler German governments was no greater than elsewhere; indeed on one occasion the president of the Reichsbank, Dr. Hans Luther, even prevailed upon Keynes to cancel a speech he had agreed to make in Berlin.[26]

In France, Keynes had, if anything, a negative influence. The French detested him because of his opposition to exacting heavy

[25] Frances Perkins, *The Roosevelt I Knew* (New York: Viking Press, 1946), pp. 225–226; J. M. Keynes to Roosevelt, February 1, 1938, Roosevelt Papers, Franklin D. Roosevelt Library, Hyde Park, N.Y.; J. M. Burns, *Roosevelt: The Lion and the Fox* (New York: Harcourt, Brace, 1956), pp. 332–333. Many American economists, however, including such important New Deal figures as Rexford G. Tugwell and Leon Henderson, were familiar with Keynes's work, and by late 1938 the Roosevelt administration was consciously applying his theories to the problems of the depression. See Robert Lekachman, *The Age of Keynes* (New York: Random House, 1968), p. 124–125.

[26] Wilhelm Grottkopf, *Die grosse Krise: Lehren aus der Überwindung der Weltwirtschaftskrise* (Düsseldorf: Econ Verlag, 1954), p. 202 n. On Keynes's influence in Germany, see especially pp. 235–239. Many Nazis later claimed that their economic policies were Keynesian in character, but this was not the case. See Claude William Guillebaud, *The Economic Recovery of Germany from 1933 to the Incorporation of Austria in March, 1938* (London: Macmillan, 1939), p. 215; Arthur Schweitzer, *Big Business in the Third Reich* (Bloomington: Indiana University Press, 1964), pp. 342–352; René Erbe, *Die nationalsozialistiche Wirtschaftspolitik im Lichte der modernen Theorie* (Zurich: Polygraphischer Verlag, 1958), passim.

reparations from Germany after World War I, which he had predicted in his best-selling book, *The Economic Consequences of the Peace* (1920), could never be collected. The depression, of course, proved the accuracy of his prediction and set the French more adamantly against his economic theories. None of his important economic writings was even translated into French until after the outbreak of World War II. In general, French politicians were, if possible, more ignorant of economic realities than were politicians of other nations. Even the Socialist leader, Léon Blum, who was almost unique among French leaders in being favorably disposed toward the American New Deal, was ignorant of Keynes's work and had a poor grasp of the most elementary economics. The economic historian Alfred Sauvy, summing up a discussion of the views of the French statesmen of the thirties, writes of their ignorance both of theory and of economic facts. "The politicians of the extreme left," he adds, "while themselves erring both in observing and interpreting reality, nevertheless continued to condemn the [capitalist] politicians for not knowing how to manipulate the economy."[27]

Yet, despite the unprecedented seriousness of the depression and the general ineptness and indecisiveness of established authority, millions suffered its burdens and indignities passively. Radicals deplored, denounced, and demanded, yet relatively few victims of the depression paid them heed. Why did radicalism fail, as it assuredly did? Only in Germany were truly radical

[27] Charles Rist, et al., *L'Enseignement économique en France et à l'étranger* (Paris: Sirey, 1937), pp. 5–30, 180–191; Colton, *Blum*, p. 179; Maurice Vaïsse, "Le Mythe de l'or en France," *Revue d'Histoire Moderne et Contemporaine* 16 (1969): 465; Sauvy, *Histoire économique*, II: 350, 352, 364. The only work of Keynes's that appeared in French before 1940 was his *Monetary Reform* (1923). See John Maynard Keynes, *Théorie générale de l'emploi, de l'intérêt, et de la monnaie* [August, 1939], tr., with an introduction by Jean de Largentaye (Paris, 1970).

measures introduced, and the German upheaval was a revolution of the Right, not of the Left. The Great Depression was a cause of the Nazi seizure of power—one of several—but it made Nazis not, in the main, of the suffering poor, but of shopkeepers, small property owners, and (eventually) of the great tycoons and landlords, groups more concerned with holding onto what they had than with rectifying social wrongs. Elsewhere the depression led to change, to various liberal reforms, but to no drastic upheaval of the status quo. When the world economy was at last resuscitated by the outbreak of World War II in 1939, the reform period that we call the New Deal was already over even in Franklin Roosevelt's eyes, although more than nine million American workers were still unemployed. Neville Chamberlain was prime minister of Great Britain, heading a thoroughly conservative government,[28] and in France, Premier Édouard Daladier presided over the same kind of center coalition that had ruled the nation when the depression began.

I can here only suggest in outline the many reasons why the Great Depression did nòt produce more genuinely radical changes in the Western world. It was, to begin with, an almost worldwide phenomenon, a cataclysm so massive and pervasive as to seem an act of Nature, like the Deluge of myth, or the great plagues of the Middle Ages, and, as such, beyond human control. It would be difficult to organize a revolt against an earthquake or to rouse those whose property has been destroyed in a tidal wave against their fellows who live on higher ground. The depression also stifled radicalism because it was so frightening. In all the industrial nations, governments, no doubt in part because of their awareness of the inadequacies of their own policies, often cracked

[28] It was, as the historian A. J. P. Taylor put it, "a humdrum government," the "'old gang' slightly reshuffled," headed by "a meticulous housemaid" (*English History*, pp. 497–498).

down hard on extremist protesters. But fear can lead to paralysis as well as to aggression. With so many unemployed, those who still held jobs were afraid of losing them and were thus unlikely to give tongue to criticism of the system, whatever their beliefs. Among the unemployed, the depression produced a great deal of violence, but also much passivity; it is a cruel fact that the more one suffered the more one was likely to become apathetic. When radicals organized, those whose interests they threatened were afraid, but they tended to fight back. Those to whom radicals appealed were often too physically and mentally debilitated to do anything at all.

In the depths of the depression the radical writer Matthew Josephson interviewed numbers of unemployed men in New York City as a correspondent of the *New Republic*. He found them, by and large, resigned, withdrawn, weak and tired from malnutrition, ashamed of their state rather than angry. When he asked the residents of a dreadful municipal shelter why they did not protest against the conditions there, they replied: "We don't dare complain about anything. We're afraid of being kicked out."

Josephson's impressions are typical of those of most observers. The effects of unemployment on individual personality were widely studied during the thirties. Investigators in the United States, England, Scotland, Germany, Austria, Belgium, Czechoslovakia, Italy, and Poland discovered that, while all men did not react to unemployment in the same way, the tendency was to be afraid, to develop feelings of inferiority, to lose hope, to become distrustful of others, and to withdraw from society. The social scientists, often in spite of their preconceptions, found that few of the unemployed were social radicals and that the longer men remained out of work the less likely they were to protest actively against their fate. The pattern was to proceed from shock when

104

the job was lost to feverish search for a new one, to pessimism
and acute psychic distress, to fatalistic acceptance of a circum-
scribed existence—apathetic, acquiescent, broken.[29]

Furthermore, radicals and reformers were divided among themselves. While, as I have said, economists offered many useful suggestions about what should be done, they differed over details,
and the area of their agreement seems clearer in retrospect than
it did at the time. And some of the most prestigious among them
held fast to classical laissez-faire ideas. These conservative economists pointed out the real difficulties involved in economic
planning; they insisted that only international efforts could cure
the depression and that too great reliance on the state—as seen in
fascism, with its stress on autarchy and ultranationalism—was a
threat to freedom. Thus liberal statesmen are not entirely to be
blamed for hesitating to adopt drastic measures—the babel of
voices urging them to move in this direction, in that one, or in
still another was most confusing.[30]

The Left was, throughout the period, split into Socialist and
Communist camps, thus its force was considerably diluted. In the
early years of the depression the Communists would support no
policy aimed at ameliorating economic conditions. They pre-

---

[29] Josephson, *Infidel*, pp. 75–80. The literature on unemployment
studies is summarized in P. Eisenberg and P. F. Lazarsfeld, "The
Psychological Effects of Unemployment," *Psychological Bulletin* 35
(1938): 358–390. Of the major investigations, the most interesting is
Jahoda, *Die Arbeitslosen von Marienthal*. See also E. W. Bakke, *The
Unemployed Man: A Social Study* (London: Nisbet and Co., 1933);
Edward A. Rundquist and Raymond E. Sletto, *Personality in the De-
pression: A Study in the Measurement of Attitudes* (Minneapolis:
University of Minnesota Press, 1936); Ewan Clague and Webster
Powell, *Ten Thousand Out of Work* (Philadelphia: University of
Pennsylvania Press, 1933); R. Kollar, et al., *Der Einfluss der Krise auf
Familien beschäftungslose Arbeiter* (Prague: Forschungstelle des Sozial-
instituts, 1933); and *Men Without Work: A Report*.

[30] See especially Robbins, *The Great Depression*, pp. 169–200.

ferred to stir up trouble and wait while capitalism went through its death throes, smugly pointing to the Soviet Union, where, under the first Five Year Plan, unemployment did not exist and output (admittedly from a very low base) was increasing while the rest of the world wallowed in depression. After the Nazi revolution in Germany, however, the various Communist parties changed their tune, calling for a Popular Front against fascism and demanding that social and economic reform be subordinated to rearmament and defense.[31]

The Socialists, besides seldom agreeing with the Communists about tactics, also failed to meet the economic challenge of the depression. Although not significant in the United States, in Europe the Socialist parties were very important. The Labour party in Great Britain was in control of Parliament during the early stages of the depression. Socialists formed the largest single party in France all through the thirties—and in Germany, as well, until Hitler snuffed out opposition parties in 1933. The intellectual bankruptcy of the British Socialists has already been mentioned. They were concerned about the unemployed to the extent that they resisted efforts to reduce relief payments, but in power they took no steps to reduce unemployment itself. Labour party leaders were uninspired therefore uninspiring, without energy therefore ineffective, lacking in courage therefore irresolute. They believed that capitalism was doomed yet knew that the nation was not psychologically ready for socialism. Thus they governed, but without conviction, pursuing a "policy of negation."

The German Socialist party (Sozialdemokratische Partei Deutschlands, or SPD) which headed the so-called Grand Coali-

---

[31] The German Communists, despite their talk about resisting fascism, actually aided the Nazis' work of undermining the republic on the fatuous theory that the destruction of democratic government would open the way to Communist revolution (Bracher, *German Dictatorship*, p. 198).

tion government from 1928 until 1930, was, like its British counterpart, overcommitted to protecting unemployment benefits and the standard of living of workers, so much so that it preferred destroying the Grand Coalition and surrendering leadership of the nation to accepting a ½ per cent increase in the unemployment-insurance tax paid by workers. Thereafter, while the depression deepened and the Nazis fattened in an atmosphere of social and economic collapse, the SPD, as the German historian Erich Mattias writes, "escape[d] into noisy opposition without tangible aims," their leaders convinced that no "general recipe" for restoring prosperity could be found. Thus the party, despite its solid seven million followers, played almost no role at all in the crucial political struggles culminating in Hitler's seizure of power.[32]

The destruction of German socialism by the Nazis greatly affected the Socialists of France. French Socialists were, like the English and Germans, unable to devise constructive policies aimed at dealing with the depression. Their leading figure, Léon Blum, could envisage' no "solution" other than socialism, and he recognized that the majority of Frenchmen were unprepared for that. He and a majority of the Socialist leaders repeatedly refused posts in centrist cabinets. They would "exercise power"

---

[32] Erich Mattias, "Social Democracy and the Power of the State," in *The Road to Dictatorship: Germany, 1918–1933*, Theodore Eschenburg, et al. (London: O. Wolff, 1964), pp. 62, 65; W. Campbell Balfour, "British Labour from the Great Depression to the Second World War"; *Mouvements ouvriers et dépression économique de 1929 à 1939*, edited by Denise Fauvel-Rouif (Assen: Van Gorcum, 1966), pp. 234–243; Skidelsky, *Politicians and the Slump*, pp. 384–395; W. Conze, "La Crise économique et le mouvement ouvrier en Allemagne entre 1929 et 1933," in *Mouvements ouvriers*, edited by D. Fauvel-Rouif, pp. 37–58. Bracher puts it this way: "The crisis-ridden trade unions pushed the SPD out of an unpopular government and steered it into a still more unpopular course of acquiescence devoid of all possibility of exerting political leverage" (*German Dictatorship*, p. 171).

in a coalition government—that is, join a coalition headed by a Socialist premier—but not accept responsibility for governing under a premier of a different party.[33]

However, the Nazi triumph and the rising militancy of fascist groups in France drove the various Socialist factions and the French Communist party into a united front against fascism, the so-called Rassemblement Populaire which produced in the elections of 1936 the Popular Front government, with Blum as premier.[34] This government, pushed by French workers in that spontaneous, joyous outburst, the sitdown strikes of June, 1936, enacted a flurry of social and economic reforms. But Blum had a scrupulous regard for legal punctilio—he refused to try to establish a Socialist system because he had not campaigned on a Socialist platform. Many radicals in his party were furious with him. "In the face of a dangerous enemy," Marceau Pivert declaimed, "he displayed the aristocratic elegance of a duellist in lace cuffs." Instead of producing the red terror that conservatives had feared, the Popular Front settled for what French capitalists were soon contemptuously calling a "*terreur rose*."[35]

[33] Georges Lefranc, *Le Mouvement socialiste sous la Troisième République* (Paris: Payot, 1963), pp. 267, 288, 294; Colton, *Blum*, pp. 71, 76–77, 90–91. Right-wing "neo-Socialists" opposed this policy, fearing that it would drive middle-class liberals to the right and working-class radicals to the left (Lefranc, *Le Mouvement socialiste*, pp. 267, 303–304).

[34] The Communists refused to hold office under Blum, but their deputies supported his government in the assembly. Maurice Thorez, the Communist leader, called the Popular Front "a contract between the working class and the middle class" against fascism (Lefranc, *Front Populaire*, p. 139).

[35] Ibid., p. 140; Bourdin, *Léon Blum*, pp. 63–64. "Everything is possible," Pivert insisted in a widely discussed article in the *Populaire de Paris*. The people "will not settle for a mere cup of insipid herb tea [*une modeste tisane de guimauve*] carried on tiptoe to the bedside of the sick mother." They are ready for "the most risky surgery"—nationalization of banks, utilities, and large corporations, confiscation of the prop-

Moreover, the Popular Front reforms did not end the depression or even lessen its baneful effects. The gains made by French workers were more social and psychological than economic—principally shorter hours and paid vacations. (One French historian even suggests that unconsciously the sitdown strikers were more concerned with achieving a style of life like that of the middle class than with improving their standard of living per se.) In any case, Léon Blum equated strong government controls with fascist totalitarianism; his public works program was pitifully inadequate; he failed to obtain a thoroughgoing reform of the Bank of France or to reduce the level of unemployment. Production actually declined. He was as incapable of escaping the budget-balancing, economy-in-government style of thought as any of his "capitalist" predecessors, and gave no more heed to the new economics than other Frenchmen. Summing up Blum's economic ideas, the historian Alfred Sauvy writes: "His ignorance of the most elementary facts was only equalled by his sincerity." French socialism thus proved to be as bankrupt in the area of economic thought as the British and German variety.[36]

Finally, despite the suffering and ineptitude I have been describing, there were important positive forces at work in most of the Western nations that blunted the economic impact of the depression and soothed the indignation of its victims. It goes without saying, for example, that patriotism remained a powerful social cement and that in some perverse way mass suffering held people together as much as it generated resentment and discon-

---

erty of capitalists who illegally export gold, and so forth. Pivert's essay is conveniently reprinted in Lefranc, *Front Populaire*, pp. 451–453.

[36] R. Dufraisse, "Le Mouvement ouvrier français 'rouge' devant la grande dépression économique," in *Mouvements ouvriers*, edited by Fauvel-Rouif, p. 172; Colton, *Blum*, pp. 182–193, 278–281; Lefranc, *Front Populaire*, pp. 314, 319–321, 341; Sauvy, *Histoire économique*, II, 303.

tent. The astonishing success in Great Britain of Noel Coward's play and movie *Cavalcade* (1932), with its bittersweet evocation of the English past, and of the American song, "Brother Can You Spare a Dime," literally pessimistic but somehow inspiring, are well-known illustrations of this phenomenon. When the British government went to vast expense to celebrate George V's Twenty-fifth Jubilee in 1936, the king himself expressed concern about spending so much public money on display, but huge crowds turned out to hail the monarch, the general atmosphere of the celebrations was exceptionally cheerful, and in the poorest sections of London men carried banners reading "Lousy but Loyal." National commitment to the Third Republic and to the ideals, however divorced from contemporary reality, of the French Revolution, served a similar function in France. Of the industrial nations, only in Germany was this sentiment lacking, or at least extremely weak, and this was certainly a major cause of the collapse of the Weimar Republic.[37]

There were also economic reasons why many resisted radical solutions to the depression. Because of the profound and widespread fall of *prices*, workers who were fortunate enough to hold onto their jobs suffered little or no decline in their standard of living. "It is significant," the League of Nations reported in 1932, "that, despite the overwhelming nature of the depression and its costs, money rates of wages in most countries have not fallen as fast as the cost of living. . . . Real wages . . . show such a general tendency to rise that there can be little doubt that most wage-earners in constant full-time employment at standard rates are . . . in a much better position than in 1929." League statistics

[37] Graves, *Long Weekend*, pp. 296–297; Harold Nicolson, *King George the Fifth: His Life and Reign* (London: Pan Books, 1967), pp. 669–672; Gay, *Weimar Culture*, pp. 17–25, 70–72, 77, 139–140; Dufraisse, "Mouvement ouvrier français," in *Mouvements ouvriers*, edited by Fauvel-Rouif, pp. 179–183.

show that at the end of 1932 the real wages of industrial workers in eleven major countries had risen between 2 and 15 per cent since 1928. They continued to go up even when prices began to rise in the middle thirties.[38]

Individual and organized private relief efforts were also important in maintaining the established order. Reactionaries and doctrinaire laissez-faire economists might insist, as the multimillionaire secretary of the treasury Andrew Mellon is said to have told President Hoover, that it was necessary to "liquidate" workers and farmers in order to "purge the rottenness out of the system," a process that Mellon apparently believed would encourage people to "work harder" and "live a more moral life." But in nearly every stricken community heroic efforts to aid the unfortunate were undertaken. In the bleak year of 1931, the national Community Chest drive in the United States collected $100 million, 25 per cent more than in the boom year of 1928. A group of prominent businessmen in New York City raised over $8 million for relief in the fall of 1930, and in 1932 private and semipublic contributions in New York totaled almost $21 million. The Community Fund of Muncie, Indiana, the "Middletown" of Robert and Helen Lynd's famous studies, raised its collections from $80,000 in 1929 to $115,000 in 1931.[39] Of course similar efforts were also characteristic of communities in Great Britain, France, and Germany.[40] Discussions of private at-

[38] League of Nations, *Economic Survey, 1932–33*, pp. 32–33, 103, 106; ibid., *1934–35* (Geneva, 1935), p. 134; ibid., *1935–36* (Geneva, 1936), pp. 75–80, 141. However, the decline in overtime work and the tendency toward part-time employment did reduce the real incomes of many who were not technically unemployed.

[39] Hoover, *Memoirs*, p. 30; A. L. Romasco, *The Poverty of Abundance: Hoover, the Nation, the Depression* (New York: Oxford University Press, 1965), pp. 151–153, 157; Robert and Helen Lynd, *Middletown in Transition* (New York, 1937), pp. 112–113.

[40] See, for example, Allen, *Nazi Seizure of Power*, pp. 67–68, 231.

tempts to aid the victims of the depression tend to stress their inadequacy, and inadequate they certainly were, but the mollifying effects of humanitarian efforts were probably large.

Far more important were the various government relief and insurance programs. When the depression struck, the United States had no national unemployment or social security laws, and President Hoover's stubborn insistence that public relief must for constitutional reasons be handled by state and municipal authorities goes far toward explaining his overwhelming defeat in the election of 1932. State and local governments proved unable to meet the enormous demand for relief, but most of them exhausted their resources trying to do so, aiding millions of sufferers in the process. By the fall of 1932, money was being provided at a rate of over $50 million a month. After Franklin Roosevelt took office, the federal government began supplying billions in direct relief and also developed its extensive public works programs, thus putting millions of unemployed to work. Critics charged that much of the work done was wasteful and coined the word "boondoggle" to express their contempt for the system, but New Deal aid for the unemployed contributed heavily to Roosevelt's popularity and to the failure of radicals to make great inroads among them.[41]

The European industrial nations had systems of social insur-

Even the Nazis developed a Winter Aid (*Winterhilfe*) program and organized soup kitchens to feed the hungry.

[41] The Germans called such projects "pyramid building." With characteristic boldness, Keynes defended public spending of this type without regard for the usefulness of the projects. "If the Treasury would fill old bottles with banknotes, bury them . . . in disused coal mines which are then filled up to the surface with town rubbish, and leave it to private enterprise on well-tried principles of *laissez-faire* to dig the notes up again . . . there need be no more unemployment" (J. M. Keynes, *The General Theory of Employment, Interest, and Money* [New York: Macmillan, 1936], p. 129).

ance long before the onset of the depression. In Great Britain, a broad scheme of unemployment insurance was established before World War I and, when chronic unemployment became a problem, the law was modified to provide "uncovenanted" or "extended" payments to those who had exhausted the benefits on their contributions. This system, known as the dole, was instituted in 1921 and extended to all unemployed persons "genuinely seeking work" in 1927. The German system, which also combined contributory unemployment insurance and lesser noncontributory poor-relief payments for those who had exhausted their benefits, was set up in 1926. France had a much less comprehensive system, based on municipal commissions made up of local officials, employers, and workers, with 60 per cent of the relief funds provided by the central government.[42]

The strains that the depression put on these systems caused much bitterness, it is true, but surely the help they brought to millions of persons aided in preventing radical changes. The tendency, world-wide, was toward a broader acceptance of public responsibility for the protection of the victims of the depression. This served to moderate discontent.[43] And as I have said, the suffering experienced by so many itself often brought societies closer together, producing what amounted to mass movements to preserve common goals and values rather than to alter insti-

[42] Eveline Mabel Richardson Burns, *British Unemployment Programs, 1920–1938: A Report Prepared for the Committee on Social Security* (Washington, D.C.: Committee on Social Security, Social Science Research Council, 1941), pp. 4–7, 40–51. The "genuinely seeking work" requirement was eliminated in 1930 and the system was further modified in 1931 and again in 1935 (Daclin, *Crise des années 30*, pp. 84–87; Gustav Stolper, et al., *The German Economy, 1870 to the Present* [New York: Harcourt, Brace, 1967], p. 106).

[43] League of Nations, *Economic Survey, 1935–36*, p. 149. Unemployment insurance and public works programs also benefited the employed by strengthening unions and increasing the competition for labor. See ibid., *1934–35*, p. 134.

tutions radically. This was the spirit of the American New Deal and of the wave of hope that swept across France after the victory of the Popular Front in the election of 1936. It was even, it must be admitted, the spirit of Hitler's National Socialists, who, however perverted their aims and cruel their methods, were fanatically committed to restoring a sense of community (*Gemeinschaft*) among Germans.[44]

This sense of participation was a fragile thing. In France it subsided as swiftly as it had arisen and the inability to keep it alive was one of Léon Blum's greatest failures and a cause of the ignominious collapse of France before Hitler's invading Panzer divisions in 1940. In Great Britain it existed throughout the depression, under the surface, probably nurtured more by tradition and the average Englishman's sense of being an islander than by any government policy or the personality of any leader. It emerged only at the time of the heroic evacuation of Dunkirk in 1940 and flowered in response to the great German air raids and Winston Churchill's magnificent rhetoric.

Today's radicals fail to take this aspect of the depression into account when they scoff at the inadequacies of, for example, the New Deal. It is of course true that Roosevelt never "solved" the unemployment problem, nor did he substantially reduce the percentage of the population that, in his own dramatic phrase, was "ill-housed, ill-clad, ill-nourished," nor did he even try to do away with racial discrimination, although American blacks were the worst sufferers of the depression. But the blacks, the poor, and the unemployed voted overwhelmingly for Roosevelt, and not because, as the modern radicals would have it, they were

[44] The historically and biologically absurd Nazi definition of "German" and the vicious tactic of seeking to unite "Germans" by turning them against Jews and other supposed "inferior" groups were, of course, the major evils of Nazism. But it would be blindness to ignore the effectiveness of this aspect of the system in mobilizing society for fighting the depression.

"seduced" by his "rhetoric."[45] New Deal efforts, however incompletely successful, gave the victims of the depression a sense of being part of a massive national struggle, and while there was indeed a rhetorical component to the New Deal—the famous Blue Eagle of NRA and its banal slogan "We Do Our Part" come to mind—rhetoric had little to do with its impact on the American people.

In sum, or so at least it seems to me, the Great Depression was a radical event and also one that exposed radical weaknesses in the capitalist system. It radicalized many persons all over the world. The depression also led to enormous changes. But these changes were not in the main basic changes, and those that were in any sense fundamental came so slowly that they can better be described as having evolved than as having arrived in a radical or revolutionary manner. They were also produced as much by World War II as by the "Great Crisis" that Eugen Varga and so many other radicals of the thirties denounced. These radicals failed to achieve nearly all their goals; the "system" (patched up, modernized, reformed) exists today essentially as before. Whether one finds in their failure reason to rejoice or despair is, I suppose, a matter of one's individual temperament and social philosophy.

[45] Barton J. Bernstein, ed., *Towards a New Past: Dissenting Essays in American History* (New York: Pantheon Books, 1968), pp. 263–288.